RIVER CAMPING

Touring by Canoe, Raft, Kayak, and Dory

by Verne Huser
Photographs by R. Valentine Atkinson

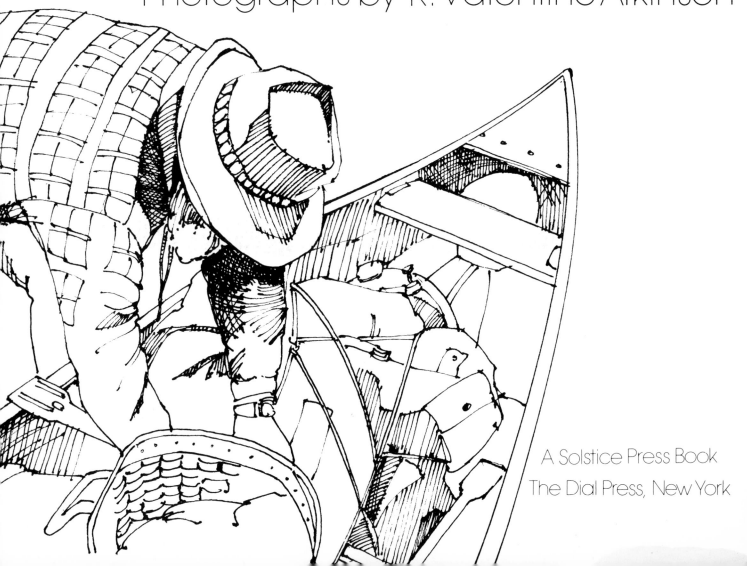

A Solstice Press Book

The Dial Press, New York

Dedicated to Willa, whom I met through
a river trip, married on the Snake River in
Hells Canyon, and have since journeyed
with on many enjoyable rivers.

Published by
The Dial Press
1 Dag Hammarskjold Plaza
New York, New York 10017

© 1981 by North Country Book Express, Inc.

Aldo Leopold's quotations from *A Sand County Almanac* are used with permission of Oxford University Press and Sheila Mill's recipe from *Rocky Mountain Kettle Cuisine* is used with permission of Galley Impressions.

All photographs in this book were taken by R. Valentine Atkinson except those credited on page 150.

A Solstice Press book produced at North Country Book Express, Moscow, Idaho, by Ivar Nelson and Patricia Hart.

Designed by Dana Sloan

Manufactured in the United States of America
First Printing

Library of Congress Cataloging in Publication Data

Huser, Verne
    River camping

    "A Solstice Press book."
    Bibliography: p.
    1. Boats and boating—United States. 2. Camping—United States. 3. Rivers—United States—Recreational use. 4. Boats and boating—Canada. 5. Camping—Canada. 6. Rivers—Canada—Recreational use. I. Title.
GV776.A2H866   917.3   81-84

ISBN 0-8037-7256-4

Preface

Aldo Leopold wrote in *A Sand County Almanac:* "We abuse land because we regard it as a commodity belonging to us. When we see land as a community to which we belong, we may begin to use it with love and respect." I hope we use our rivers with love and respect, with a sense of responsibility for our own actions as well as a sense of respect for other people.

When we run rivers, we become a part of the river community. For all of our good intentions, however, we may simply not know how to treat the river world kindly. Unknowingly we follow established patterns and continue to treat the river as a commodity.

There has been an explosion in recreational river use during the past decade. That popularity influenced me to write this book. Because of that explosion, especially among inexperienced river users, we are losing the quality of the river experience. We are loving our rivers to death.

And it does not have to be. The impact of river camping is threatening to destroy many areas. While some of our rivers are being overused, it is not the amount of use so much as the kind of use which stimulated me to write a book about river camping. I believe that North American rivers can withstand more use today than a few years ago because we are learning to take better care of them.

The Grand Canyon is cleaner now than in 1968, largely due to new camping policies enforced by the National Park Service. But sensible river camping practices should not have to be enforced. I don't like regulations, but unless we regulate our own use of the river resource, we are asking to be regulated by others.

It is my purpose in writing this book to help inform people of the principles of minimal impact camping and its practical applications. We should leave so little evidence of our passage that the next party will not even suspect that we were there. When we dip our paddles or oars into the water and take a stroke, the action leaves little permanent impact on the river. We should treat the land in the same way. The land does not recover as quickly as the river. Up to now, we have greatly reduced its capacity to renew itself.

Let us all learn to use our rivers without destroying their appeal or reducing their capacity to tolerate our presence. I would like for my children to enjoy some of the experiences I have known camping along North American waterways.

I wish to thank the many people whose information and counsel have helped make this book. If the book contributes to preserving the river experience we share, that is the best thanks I can offer. Eric Evans and Rod Nash were especially generous to review the manuscript, as were Rod and Roger Drayna to help organize our trips on which Valentine Atkinson took his wonderful photographs.

Verne Huser
December 1980
Redmond, Washington

Contents

THE RIVER

Labyrinth Canyon, named by John Wesley Powell, who first explored it, is a deep gash in the red-rock country of southeastern Utah. Fleecy fair-weather clouds drifting overhead have pink bottoms, color reflected off the desert sandstone. The Green River flows unhurriedly between its canyon walls decorated with ancient petroglyphs along sandbars gone green with tamarisk. Dennis Julian left his mark in the canyon in 1836. Uranium explorers more than a century later left their mark too.

An idyllic canoe route, this lovely river is home to beaver and boatmen, a recreational highway every Memorial Day for the Annual Friendship Cruise that opens the boating season in Utah. If any stretch of river in North America deserves to be protected, this stretch of the Green does. But it may never be. It has too many other values that have higher priority, at least in the eyes of the people in power in Utah and in the nation: values such as minerals, power potential, water for energy development, and irrigation.

Rivers are many things to many people. To the miner, rivers are a source of mineral wealth. To the farmer/rancher, rivers are a source of water for livestock and for crops and hay fields. To the fishery biologist, rivers are habitat. To the fishing guide, a source of income. To the small boy, a place to fish. To the engineer, a source of untapped power. To the construction worker, a source of aggregate. To the historian, the route of the Oregon Trail or the voyageurs.

The river is a composite of resources which are viewed differently by various special interests. A constant battle rages over the best use of the river between consumptive uses, which provide jobs but prohibit other uses, and more neutral activities which leave little trace of their passing.

Paddle up the North River from Willapa Bay as the tide comes in, and feel the surge of the sea that helps propel you into the wilderness, where you approach a drinking deer so silently that undisturbed, it merely returns your gaze as you float by, water dripping from its soft muzzle.

A thousand ducks rise from the river as you launch into the clear water of the silt-free Colorado at Lee's Ferry for a two-week run of the Grand Canyon. After the tributary Paria enters downriver, the water is muddy brown from the silt. Your stomach mildly churns because you know you will have to face Hance Rapid in a few days, then Crystal, and ultimately Lava Falls, the great granddaddy of them all. There is a vague uneasiness in anticipation of the big drops, but as the dark walls (darker in memory than in fact) close in about you, you give your soul to the canyon for half-a-month, and thrill at what lies ahead.

The bush pilot disappears in the distance, leaving you and your small party (even smaller, it seems, with the last link to civilization gone) to launch on a crystal-clear Brooks Range river in the living heart of northern Alaska where the fishing is great but so are the bears, and there is no one to help you if you get into trouble.

Flow

The flow of water in the river determines if the river is runnable. It suggests what kind of craft is best and how experienced you have to be. Water levels do vary with snowmelt, rain, and reservoir release. Sudden drops and rises will affect both river running and camping on the banks. At high levels, the flow is fast and the water is usually cold. At low levels, the flow is slower and more rocks and logs are exposed. Some rapids are drowned out at high water and others become unrunnable. You need to know the river at all levels to run it safely.

Flow is measured in cubic feet per second (cfs). Cfs levels are meaningless unless related to what the river is like at various levels. You can get official water level readings, but your best information will probably come from other river runners or from personal inspection. In some areas, water level is measured in vertical feet at a given point.

International Difficulty Scale

Most rivers do not drop at a constant rate but rather in steps. The overall drop may be twelve feet per mile, but if the fall comes in two separate drops of six feet, you could have some problems.

A commonly heard phrase on whitewater rivers is "go with the flow." It urges river runners to move with the current, and not to fight the river. You learn about flow by experiencing it, by watching rivers, and by being thrashed a time or two.

The most common rating scale for rivers is the International Scale of River Difficulty reproduced here. It is used in Europe and North America and ranges from I to VI, with VI being unrunnable. A second classification system used on many big-water rivers, especially in the western United States, has a ten-point scale.

Ratings will vary with different water levels. Rapids can be created overnight by changes in flow or landslides. Rivers, or segments of rivers, are often classified as well, based on the difficulty of their rapids. That practice can be misleading if the rating is justified by only a few rapids which could be lined or portaged.

Class I Easy moving water with minimal obstacles, small waves.

Class II Easy rapids with waves up to three feet, wide, clear, obvious channels, some maneuvering required but no scouting.

Class III Rapids with high, irregular waves capable of swamping an open canoe, narrow passages requiring complex maneuvers and possible scouting from shore.

Class IV Long, difficult rapids with constricted passages that require precise maneuvering in very turbulent water. Scouting is necessary and rescue may be difficult. *Generally not possible for open canoes.*

Class V Extremely difficult long, violent rapids with congested routes requiring scouting from shore and precise moves. Rescue is difficult, and there is significant hazard to life. Eskimo roll is essential for kayaks and decked canoes. Paddle rafts are at the very edge of possibility.

Class VI Difficulties of Class V carried to the extreme of navigability. Nearly impossible and very dangerous. For teams of experts only.

Geology

Rivers have created much of the North American continent and have carved much of its most impressive features. Sediment laid down by prehistoric rivers solidified. More recent rivers have cut anew through those pages of earth history (witness the Great Unconformity in the Grand Canyon). Ancient metamorphic rocks have been exposed by glaciers, rivers of ice which carve the land with their melting, creating new rivers. Igneous (fire-formed) formations line many rivers with columnar basalt (hexagonal columns of lava) or exfoliating (flaking off) granite, products of heat from underground activity.

John Wesley Powell, a geologist who first explored the Grand Canyon, reflecting on the great "conflict of water and fire" when a volcanic flow dammed the Colorado River tens of thousands of years ago, wrote: "Just imagine a river of molten rock running down into a river of melted snow." Lava Falls, one of the most feared rapids in the West, is the result.

Frost action quarries living rock from the mountain. Gravity and snowmelt carry the rock downstream, chipping away at the rough edges, creating gravel and grains of sand which line the river bottom and form bars that alter the river's course. The river begins to meander in mountain meadows and broad valleys, looping back on itself, even short-cutting itself to leave isolated oxbows.

Geologic principles come alive when you drift beneath the towering glaciers of the St. Elias Range on the Tatshenshini, one of the many rivers shared by Canada and the United States. They live too in the braided channels and rounded cobbles of the Snake in Jackson Hole where the Teton Range passes in spectacular review, in the cross-bedded sandstones of the Cheat in West Virginia, and in the karst topography of west Texas where spring-fed streams burst cold and clear from seemingly solid rock.

History

River history fascinates me. It has ever since I read about *coureurs du bois* and the Lewis and Clark expedition. Much American history is related to the waterways in both Canada and the United States.

The French were the earliest European explorers. Jacques Cartier (1535) discovered the St. Lawrence. Samuel de Champlain (1608) extended the exploration and settled Quebec ("where the river

narrows"). Marquette and Joliet (1673) discovered the Mississippi. Daniel Duluth (1680) opened up vast new territories looking for the fabled Northwest Passage.

Nicolet, Groseilliers, Radisson, McTavish, Pond, and the Frobishers explored further inland, opening up still more of the wilderness world to civilization. There was a newer breed of American that included George Rogers Clark and his more famous younger brother William, who teamed with Meriwether Lewis to push the claim of the fledgling United States to the Pacific via the Missouri, Clearwater, Snake, and Columbia.

There were the flatboatmen, the keelboatmen, and the mountain men who linked the developing East to the still-wild West. Steamboats began to operate during the second decade of the 19th century and played a vital role in the development of the West, only dying out when the railroads became king.

John Wesley Powell used the railroad to reach the Green River in Utah and launch his exploration of the canyons of the Green and Colorado rivers in 1869 and in 1871. Powell's expedition led to the establishment of both the United States Geological Survey and the Bureau of Reclamation (now Water and Power Resource Service).

A young Army officer, Gus Doane, explored the upper Snake in the winter of 1876-77 and later became our first Arctic explorer. John C. Fremont used an inflatable boat of "India rubber" on the Great Salt Lake in 1853.

Near the turn of the century, a beaver trapper on the Yampa and Green rivers near where Utah and Colorado join began a new style of river running. Nat Galloway, using a decked wooden boat similar to Powell's, rowed facing downstream so he could see where he was going. The river was stronger than he was, but he could control his course. The technique caught on and revolutionized river running by rowed boat.

About the same time, Harry Guleke began building wooden scows on the Salmon River in Idaho, charging passengers $1000 for passage from Salmon City to Riggins on the famed "River of No Return" that had halted the Lewis and Clark party a century earlier. Nat Galloway's son Parley, while in jail in Vernal, Utah, for poaching beaver, taught a couple of carpenters, Bus Hatch and Frank Swain, how to build a river boat. They began running rivers in Utah, Colorado, and Arizona, pioneering commercial river running during the Great Depression. They eventually made the first trip down the Middle Fork of the Salmon in 1936.

Recreational boating became tremendously popular in the eastern United States after the Civil War, largely through the efforts of John MacGregor, who imported "canoeing" from England, even though both the canoe and kayak were Native American craft. A "canoe" in England was either a canoe, a kayak, or a hybrid of the two. In Canton, New York, J. Henry Rushton began building boats in response to MacGregor's influence. Peterborough (Ontario) and Old Town (Maine) became the centers of boating activity. Rushton helped found the American Canoe Club in 1880. The canoe has been little changed until the past decade or two when new materials and new uses have led to alterations in hull design and to the decked canoe. The canoe is by far the most widely used craft on the North American continent. The kayak, developed by the Eskimo, evolved in Europe into the modern sport craft. The dory grew up largely in the Pacific Northwest as a steelhead fishing craft.

Inflatable craft, used by a mere handful of river runners (notably Amos Burg) before World War II, became popular when surplus rafts, assault boats, and pontoons were available after the war. The sportyak, developed as a dinghy, was used as a river craft by Bill Belknap and Otis (Doc) Marston for a 1963 low-water trip through the Grand Canyon for the National Park Service.

The johnboat of the South was developed to run shallow rivers and grew up with the country, its design largely a closely-kept family secret. Today the old wooden johnboat is almost gone, replaced by aluminum boats powered by motors rather than the traditional wooden pole.

Wild and Scenic Rivers

The National Wild and Scenic Rivers System was created by Congress in 1968 to preserve in a free-flowing state "certain selected rivers . . . with their immediate environments [that] possess outstandingly remarkable scenic, recreational, geologic, fish and wildlife, cultural or other similar values . . . for the benefit and enjoyment of present and future generations."

Initially, there were eight rivers in the System and 27 others in a study category for possible future addition. Since that time, 47 river segments have been added to the System (25 of these by the Alaska Lands Bill of 1980), and the study list has grown to nearly 100. The Act that created the System provides for the addition of rivers through an ongoing review process.

There are three protective categories under the System: wild, scenic, and recreational, each involving rather specific criteria and offering different levels of protection. There are three methods to protect the land adjacent to the rivers: complete public ownership; public control through scenic or other easements; and local zoning ordinances.

The System continues to grow, having increased by 40% in both the number of rivers and the length of river mileage even before the Alaska Lands Bill was signed. At this writing (winter 1980), the System includes 55 rivers in more than half of the states, a total of some 5000 miles.

Economy

Rivers have numerous economic values: gold, sand and gravel, water for irrigation and for slurry pipelines, power to be harnessed and converted into electricity, waterways for transportation, and habitats for fish and wildlife. Economic considerations play a large role in determining how to use rivers. Aldo Leopold wrote more than thirty years ago in his classic *A Sand County Almanac* that

Rivers have been major transportation routes on this continent from the days of the canoe, bullboat, dugout, and keelboat. The great tree of waterways formed by the Ohio and Missouri systems off the trunk of the Mississippi was the major route of commerce for the developing United States for a century before the railroads came.

Dams have converted many rivers into a series of impoundments that have frustrated anadromous fish in their trip to their saltwater pastures. Consumptive uses have dewatered rivers, reducing their value for boat transportation, and water has been re-routed for slurry pipelines.

In-stream flows for fish and recreation are pitted against out-of-stream flows for agricultural, industrial, and municipal uses. Consumptive uses are put in conflict with non-consumption uses. One value is juxtaposed to another in an increasing struggle as more people compete for fewer resources, less water, and limited recreational opportunities. The limiting of a resource enhances its value. Rivers and water have greater value today than ever before. Recreational uses need to be advocated in the market place as competition increases.

"One basic weakness in a conservation system based wholly on economic motives is that most members of the land community have no economic value . . . . When one of these non-economic categories is threatened, and if we happen to love it, we invent subterfuges to give it economic importance." Witness the snail darter.

Ecology

Ecology is the science that deals with the relationships among living things and their environment. It is the only science that makes sense to me because it ties all the others together and gives them meaning. The ecology of the river involves its geology, for prehistoric rivers cut away the cliffs through which the present rivers flow. It involves plant and animal life of the river and of the entire river drainage. This area extends far beyond what the river camper can see.

Thus the impacts of our actions upon the river are far-reaching, and on a local level can often be devastating. Careless river campers have started fires that have destroyed campsites for several seasons, even decades. The trampling of too many feet beats down the bank and creates paths that cause erosion.

Everything is tied to everything else, and even subtle impacts may have long-lasting implications. We must be careful because we may not know the ultimate results of our actions. We do not have to tip-toe through the campsite or carry out our dental floss (some bird might use it in a nest), but we should be aware of ecological patterns and avoid upsetting them.

Simply look around you. Observe the river world as you find it. It has a constantly changing mood. Give a yell, listen to the echo and observe the changes you have wrought. Light the morning campfire and sense what happens in the natural world of which you are a part. The river may not seem delicate as it roars through a rapid or over a falls, but delicate balances exist within the water. Certain fish thrive within specific temperature ranges and turbidity levels, and die or fail to reproduce at other ranges.

Campsite food may attract more insects to beaches, providing more food for lizards, which increase their numbers in response to a greater food supply that disappears when the recreational season ends. Bears may attack campers because previous parties have not been careful with their food and have attracted bears to the campsite as a feeding area.

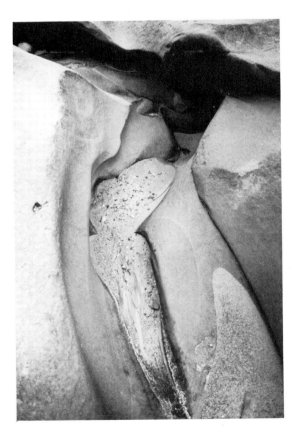

PREPARATION

What is your favorite river? It depends. The Skagit is quiet and lovely in the autumn when vine-maple red reflects in riffles shattered by spawning salmon. Canoeing the Rio Grande in Big Bend during the Christmas season can be quite pleasant. The raging big-water rapids of Cataract Canyon in the spring are an adrenaline rush caught between cold water and hot air. Cruising a barely-moving Georgia swamp in the spring is a trip of mystery into a primeval forest. Kayaking the clear, chilly whitewater of more than 250 miles of nine wonderful rivers in Jasper National Park is pure excitement.

Whichever you choose, these trips can all be delightful if time and care are devoted to proper planning and preparation. If not, they can be as miserable as a trip I took on one of my favorite rivers last summer.

I was teaching a course called "The River Resource" at the Grand Teton Environmental Education Center, and I wanted my students to see a river as it flows into a reservoir, a drowned river with all the changes that creates. We rented a raft from a commercial outfitter to run the upper Snake below Yellowstone National Park where it flows into Jackson Lake. During the negotiations by phone, something got lost in translation, and everything went wrong except the weather, which was wonderful.

We arrived at the put-in early, but the craft was not in sight nor was it an hour later. By the time it did arrive, I was so anxious to be on the river that I failed to check things carefully. The raft was soft, but I thought little of it because this was a placid stretch of river. The raft was a bit damp, but that is not too uncommon. Who minds a little water in the bilge?

So we launched. We soon discovered an inch-long slit in the bottom of the raft through which water was seeping. We had no bailing device. The raft kept getting softer and softer, but we had no pump to top it off. The river was so low and so slow that we had no time to stop but had to eat our lunch on the water. The situation became dangerous as the raft slowly turned into a wet noodle.

When I saw another raft downstream, I began rowing for all I was worth. The people in the other craft were lazing in the sun and fishing. They saw us and my wave for help, but they just waved back, not recognizing my raised oar as a distress signal. I rowed hard, finally catching up with them just before our raft became all but unmanageable.

I borrowed a pump, topped off the boat—tighter than it had been when we launched—and we shoved off again in the last bit of current before hitting the slack water of the reservoir. Using a small outboard motor, we were able to work our way through the silt bars and underwater stumps to our landing.

The trip was an adventure, less than an ideal experience, but it proved to me again the importance of careful planning and total preparation.

Which River?

I suggest starting close to home. A beer float on the Buffalo is a different experience from running the big drops in the Grand Canyon.

Some rivers can be run for only a short season, perhaps only a few weeks. Others can only be run for a week at a time because of limited access points. If you want to follow the voyageur route by canoe, the Powell route by raft, or the Lewis and Clark route by kayak, your choice of river has been made. If you are after big fish, you have many choices. If you want a wilderness experience, you have vast possibilities, but you may have to go a long way from home to pursue them. The time and money you anticipate spending will have a lot to say about which river you select. So will the season, the flow, and the travel time involved.

Don't be misled into trying one of the big-name rivers just for the prestige. There may be many other rivers closer to home that offer more of what you really want. You may find the Middle Fork of the Salmon too crowded in mid-summer for your wilderness expectations. The Grand Canyon is often full of backpackers and motorized baloney

Which Craft?

boats. The great northern rivers of Canada and Alaska can be infested by black flies and hordes of mosquitoes during certain seasons.

Do some research in magazines, books, and the travel section of newspapers. Talk to friends, distant relatives, and former classmates. Correspond with outfitters and guides. Join paddle clubs and benefit from the experience of other members. If you run rivers, you will meet other river runners who have run other rivers. You'll develop your own favorites quickly.

You might already have a favorite craft, whether you own it, rent it, or borrow it. Since you are familiar with that craft, it is probably the one to use, unless the river you want to run requires another type. Open canoes are not the best craft for heavy rapids. Rafts certainly are not the craft to use if you plan to go very far upstream, but this may be a perfect situation for johnboats or canoes powered by poles. If you will need to portage any distance, you do not want a dory or large raft. If you plan to eat well, you will want the carrying capacity of a canoe, raft, or dory — or a support craft for supplies.

Rafts and kayaks will handle the toughest whitewater. Sportyaks and dories are next in their ability to negotiate rapids. Rafts and sportyaks are poor choices for flat water. Canoes are best for flatwater rivers, but with expert paddlers, they can negotiate Class III waters handily. Johnboats are great for upstream travel. Your choice of river may be based on the craft you plan to use.

Kayaks, sportyaks, and inflatable canoes/kayaks are do-it-yourself conveyances for the individual. Canoes and kayaks (even the inflatable types) can be two-person craft, and small rafts can accommodate small groups. Johnboats and dories can carry small parties of two to four, depending upon conditions and size of the craft. Rafts come in an assortment of sizes, from eight feet long to large, 37-foot pontoons used on many big-water rivers.

A whitewater river in the Canadian Rockies may call for a kayak, while the Chattooga in Georgia and South Carolina may be best suited to a small paddle raft. A sportyak is the way to go on the San Juan in southeastern Utah. Many times a combination of craft is the best answer for a particular trip, such as a mix of rafts, dories, kayaks, and small inflatables.

The season of the year matters a great deal in planning your river trip. During spring runoff, many of the best campsites will be inundated, but there may also be very few people with whom to share them. Spring floods may keep you off the river, and when rivers of the north country experience ice floes, you don't want to be on the water. In summer you may have to put up with more people, black flies, and mosquitoes, but the weather and water are more stable, and the kids are out of school.

If you hit a streak of Indian summer in the fall, your trip can be glorious, like Hells Canyon during the first week of October in 1979, or you may run into two weeks of rain as we did on the Salmon in September of 1977. If you fish, you need to go when the season is open and the fish are running. If it is the bald eagle concentration on the upper Skagit you are after, you will be out in the winter months. Salmon runs? Autumn colors? Swimming weather? All are seasonal.

Some of the desert rivers of the Southwest run for only a few days (Escalante and Paria) or a few weeks (Dolores) each year, and some of the reservoir-release rivers can only be run during rare spills (Gauley). Those who plan to hunt will need to go when the season is open. Those who plan to find the magic mushrooms will be out in the rain. Hypothermia is a constant threat on winter trips, but flat-water trips can be fun if you dress warmly. I have canoed the upper Snake in mid-December with Dave Demaree and Frank Ewing in order to participate in the Audubon Christmas bird count.

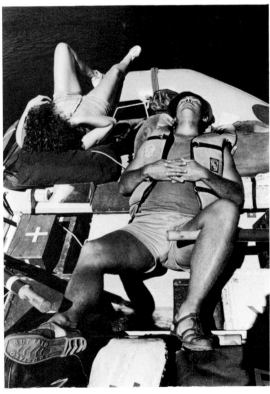

may have to send in a list of names months before your actual launch date. Early planning becomes important. It may be wise to have people of diverse talents along: a doctor, a geologist, a good fisherman, a botanist, a banjo player, an amateur astronomer, a historian, or a story teller. One member of the party may be a wiz at logistics, another at maps, and a third at cooking. One person may be a more experienced river runner while another may know the particular river better.

The Party

Who do you want to have along? It is your choice, but try to keep your party small to minimize impact on the environment. Since safety suggests no fewer than two craft in a party (preferably three), the total number of people will be from two to fifteen. I do not recommend solo trips, but many experienced paddlers take them. If a party is larger than fifteen, I begin to feel crowded. I prefer no more than ten or twelve.

On commercial trips you may not be able to pick your companions, unless you book the whole trip with your family and friends. When you plan your own trip, you can decide the party's size and composition. You will want to pick your fellow river campers carefully, especially if you plan a long trip, because you will be spending a lot of time with them. It may be wise to run a shorter, weekend shakedown trip before you invite people on your expedition to the Arctic.

It is not wise to twist people's arms to get them to go on a river trip just because they are part of the family or some other group. It could spoil the trip for everyone. Besides, there will be enough people around who really want to go. You won't have any trouble filling the trip. If you do, call me.

In the instance of rationed rivers, the party size may be limited by permit. You

Joint planning is common, but even when two or three people plan together there should be a designated leader. Leadership may be shared and specific details or responsibilities allocated, but one individual needs to oversee the total operation and pull everything together.

When co-equals river camp together, it may be awkward for one or the other to be boss, and maybe they have worked together so long that the division of labor and responsibility goes without saying. On commercial trips, the leadership is obvious. Every guide is a sub-leader of the craft he operates, but one of the guides or the outfitter will be trip leader. On private trips, the same thing should hold true, though the degree of leadership exerted will vary with the overall experience of the group. The trip on which one person is the understood, designated, or elected leader will be most successful.

Information

Information on river running and on river camping is available, but you often have to dig for it. The library is a good place to begin. So is Sources at the end of this book. Search through bookstores that cater to outdoor interests. Join a paddle club or a national organization of river runners and subscribe to their publications. Start making lists of questions and of answers as you find them.

Provincial and territorial tourist offices provide valuable information on river running throughout Canada. Write to agencies in charge of river supervision, to local chambers of commerce, to outfitters, and to other local people, if you can find any. Follow any lead. Listen for any new information. Dig out old articles and books from your own files or from your local library. Keep adding new information to your files until you head for the river.

One of the best sources of books on many aspects of river running is Westwater Books, but many outdoor mail-order outlets, water sport specialty stores, and outdoor clubs can help you. Outdoor clubs may have films, slide

shows, and personal-experience talks about river trips that will enable you to prepare yourself and meet people who organize such trips.

Planning a river camping trip requires all kinds of information about seasons, water levels, water temperatures, weather, put-ins and take-outs, schedules, and permits. Until you examine the length and difficulty of the river, the time that it takes to run a given segment, the hazards to expect, the nature of the terrain, and the level of development in the area, you really cannot begin to plan.

There is so much you cannot control on a river trip that it pays to control what you can. The best way to do that is to research the trip thoroughly and make decisions based on that information. Your research should include where the nearest source of help might be. On the Main Salmon a few years ago we had an emphysema victim whose condition grew worse on the river while the weather was deteriorating. Knowing there was an airstrip at a ranch a mile downstream from our camps, one of the guides ran to the ranch just as a plane landed with visitors. The plane waited until we could float the man down to the ranch and then flew him out to a hospital. He was receiving top medical attention in less than three hours of his first complaint.

Goods maps of both the area and the river are essential to careful planning. Guides to specific rivers are even better, though they may concentrate so heavily on the river that they offer little other information that may be important in planning.

Good area maps are produced by the U.S. Geological Survey and the Canada Map Office. There may be better maps available on specific rivers, but for general purposes, these are the ones to obtain.

Several federal agencies publish free maps of various rivers, and a number of state and provincial agencies publish guides to waterways. Readers should check out the map situation locally because it may change from year to year, just as rivers themselves may change. By researching the specific river you plan to

run, you may find a number of different maps and guides to the same area, each offering useful information lacking in another. Collect all of them. Each may save your bacon in a different way.

Maps are more useful to the river runner if they show general topography. Without contour lines it is hard to locate yourself on a map. Tributaries are useful to know, but general terrain features are, perhaps, even more important since the lay of the land is critical to the flow of the river.

In twenty-five years of river running, I have never used a compass. However, in wilderness situations, on wide rivers broken by islands, and on waterways that include lakes, the use of a compass may be vital. Orienteering Services, USA, is operated by the Silva Company (which makes good compasses). This group publishes useful (and free) educational materials and helps people learn to read maps, use compasses, and practice orienteering.

River recreation has increased so rapidly in the past decade that river use has been rationed in several popular areas. Where use has not yet been rationed, local services have sometimes been overtaxed. You need a permit to run many rivers, and that permit may be available only through a lottery. Plan your river trip early enough to apply for necessary permits and to make reservations for motels, shuttles, bush pilots, and other crucial services. To run some eastern rivers, you may need permission from private landowners. Other times, you may need to cross private land to launch, or to stay on private land to camp. Check out the details with the proper authorities and local landowners. They can often help you make reservations or get necessary permits.

For many of the more popular western rivers, you must apply for federal permits between December 1 of the previous year and January 31 of the year you plan to run. You take your chances in the lottery game. I have never won the lottery for the Middle Fork of the Salmon or for the Selway in Idaho.

It is best to check with the management agency, such as the National Park Service, Parks Canada, Bureau of Land Management, or Forest Service, for the

particular river in question. Grand Canyon is rationed. So are several Idaho and Utah rivers, and the Yampa River in Colorado. Others are rationed only for commercial use, and commercial trips fill up quickly on those rivers. For the commercial trips, too, you must get your reservations in early, sometimes a year in advance.

Many other rivers that are not rationed require permits. In most cases, this is merely a formality which enables the agency to keep track of use and inform

the river user of regulations and minimal impact camping practices. Canadian provinces and territories at this time exert little control over river use.

One of the big controversies among resource management agencies continues to be the question of allocating river use. Some users believe that all private use should be accommodated before any commercial use is allowed. Others divide the resource in half, offering 50% to private use, 50% to commercial use.

Menus

To plan food for the trip, first count the meals. List them and outline the pattern for each meal — breakfast, lunch, dinner, and snacks. Then calculate total quantities of food for the trip. On long trips, you can repeat menus. For ten days on the Salmon, we planned two five-day menus. You can have each party member, each couple, or each boat plan a meal, but one person should coordinate the food for the whole trip. Most river parties eat well because they can carry a greater variety and quantity of food than can backpackers, skiers, or cyclists.

In modern ice chests, frozen meat will keep for several days, unless the heat is excruciating. You can use dry ice or wet ice, but meat should be thawed during the day for the evening meal. Some parties will carry a chest of extra ice to add as initial ice melts. Many parties will carry no ice at all and depend upon freeze-dried foods, non-perishables, and canned goods. Weight and perishability are key factors in planning.

Menus should be well balanced, have variety, and provide plenty of fiber (from fresh fruit, vegetables, and whole cereals) and energy (from dried fruit, nuts, candy, and honey). Vegetarian menus may not require much ice for refrigeration. All meals will need staple items such as dried milk, salt, coffee and tea, sugar, perhaps eggs, Bisquick, various spices, and cooking oil. Menus may be planned for high energy, low garbage yield, ease of preparation, lightness of weight, or just plain tastiness.

Buying Food

You can turn your grocery store into a river foods store by selective buying. Many camping foods can now be purchased at the supermarket at much lower prices than can their counterparts under special backpacking labels. Soups, sauces, and gravies make good bases for river meals.

If you take a lot of river trips, you may want to buy some items in quantity. Bulk rice and granola, cases of canned goods, and peanut butter keep well. You want to buy produce just before you head to the river, but many other items can be purchased days, or even weeks, ahead. Any meats or fish to be refrigerated should be purchased frozen and kept that way until you need them. Be especially careful not to refreeze fish.

If good farm produce is available near the river, you may wait until you arrive to purchase your fresh fruits and vegetables. Wherever the price is right is the best place to buy. Food prices are especially high in Alaska, but so are air-freight rates. You may want to buy everything locally if freight costs too much or is too difficult to arrange.

Packing

Packing for the river begins to get my juices flowing. I know it's going to happen. The contemplation is almost over, and the trip is about to start. I like to pack foods by meals—dinner for one evening and breakfast for the following morning together in one pack. Lunches are separate, as they occur every day with essentially the same foods repeated and replenished, but I normally have a re-supply container for lunch items. A kitchen box contains staples like coffee, tea, hot chocolate, salt, pepper, sugar, spices, and utensils.

Bread is packed separately, or perhaps packed around eggs to prevent their cracking, or packed with heavy canned goods for weight balance. The lunch box itself contains a cutting board, knives, forks, and spoons for serving and spreading, a table cloth, and all items packed for that day's meal. Perishables may be carried in the ice chest until the lunch box is packed each day on the river or until you stop for lunch.

Outfitters

In packing the ammo cans for my raft trips or packs for my canoe trips, I always re-package as much as I can to get rid of excess weight and bulk. I use small plastic bags to keep items separated, protected, and waterproof. I pack heavy items low, pad any glass, and wrap hard external surfaces with soft items. If food containers are not waterproof, all items that might suffer from a wetting should be packed in plastic bags to keep them dry. On trips involving several rafts, I may have one ice chest with dry ice for the frozen goods, another with ice for the perishables, and a third for extra ice, beer, and soda.

Outfitters are for those people who want to run a river but either do not know how or do not have the equipment necessary to do so themselves. Ask the state or provincial tourist offices for lists of outfitters and see Sources for further information.

Outfitters can arrange guided canoe and kayak trips, do-it-yourself trips by sportyak and inflatable canoe or kayak, and many kinds of fishing and whitewater trips by raft or dory. Some of the trips are luxury cruises while others are roughing-it outings. You may go river camping for a weekend or for several weeks. (The cost per day usually drops in direct proportion to the length of the trip.) Group fees or family rates may be available, and there may be discounts for senior citizens or children. Know what you are getting for the price you are paying.

Not all outfitters offer the same quality service. It is hard to know who or what to believe unless you do some comparative shopping. To make an informed

choice, collect as much information as possible from the outfitters, from the agencies that administer their operations (if any), and from previous customers. Length of service is not necessarily a valid criterion, but if an outfitter has been around for a number of years, it is likely he can be depended upon.

Know what you want in a river trip. Outfitter brochures may help you make that decision. Learn what services, options, and possibilities there are and how much everything costs. Check for hidden costs like equipment rental fees and transportation. You will quickly learn to read between the lines of the brochures and find flaws in the fancy talk.

Ask about the kind of equipment used, the number of people per boat, the number of boats in the party, and the number of miles covered each day. Learn all you can about safety records of the outfitter and the quality of his equipment. The research you do is aimed at determining which outfitter offers the package nearest to your needs. Perhaps he can put together a special package just for you.

Training

Conditioning for any strenuous outdoor activity becomes more and more important with age. Training for river trips is important for young and old, men and women. Conditioning makes the trip more enjoyable because you don't spend half the trip being stiff and sore. You revel in your well-being and have energy to climb the hill above camp or to take an afternoon swim after spending eight or ten hours working on the river.

You will be safer and in better hands on the river trip if you and all your companions spend a few weeks getting ready physically. I do the Canadian Air Force exercises daily and have for years. When I have a major river trip coming up, I start a new routine of hiking, lifting light weights, moving the manure pile behind the barn, and making a few one-day runs on a nearby river. Exercises which toughen the hands and strengthen the wrists are desirable.

You don't have to run, row, or go to the gym to get in shape for a river trip. Just watch your diet a bit and take off a few of those extra pounds. Start (slowly) an exercise routine, do a lot of walking, and take the stairs instead of the elevator. If you like more active physical training, running is fine. So are racquet ball, handball, squash, tennis, and a number of other activities that make the heart pound and the breath come short for a while.

CRAFT

Throughout history, log rafts and skin boats were used for crossing rivers and transporting people and goods. The Nez Perce Indians used log rafts for ferrying their possessions across the spring snowmelt floodwaters of the Snake in Hells Canyon in 1877 after being driven from their homelands in the Wallowa Valley of northeastern Oregon. Indians of the high western plains used bullboats made of buffalo hides, while those of the northern woods used moose-hide or caribou-hide boats of similar construction. The skin was stretched over a sapling frame and caulked with tallow or pine sap.

The original kayak was made of sealskin and the larger open umiak of walrus skin sewn together and treated with oil to waterproof the seams. Dugouts were the earliest canoes and were made of hollowed-out logs. Before the European invasion of North America, native inhabitants made excellent canoes from the bark of trees stretched over frames of tough, pliable wood. For details of that classic craft, get John McPhee's *The Survival of the Bark Canoe.* It is delightful reading.

Just as primitive peoples designed boats from materials at hand, so modern sportsmen have made use of available materials to develop their sport by converting fishing vessels and wartime craft into river boats. The inflatables' ancestors were born before history began, but they developed to their present form through wartime technology in the early 1940s, as did the use of aluminum for various hard-hulled craft.

Craft design and construction technique have been altered drastically in recent history by synthetic fabrics. The keel is being dropped on most recreational river craft. Special hull designs have taken its place except where it is essential to hold the craft together. All inflatables are now made of synthetic fabrics. Wood has been largely replaced by fiberglass, aluminum, or modern plastics for most hard-hulled craft, although traditional dories, johnboats, and canoes are still hand-crafted by boat lovers.

Flotation has come into general use during the past few decades as a safety measure to keep craft afloat when capsized or swamped. River-worthy inflatables will float with their bottoms cut out. The more air chambers in the support tubes, the safer the craft. Some of the new synthetics, which consist of a layer of foam sandwiched between layers of tough outer fabric, also add to flotation.

Flotation has been built into most modern hard-hulled craft, either with airtight chambers (as in the sportyak) or with some lightweight high-volume material. Whitewater craft should have extra flotation added. You can use inner tubes inflated and tied into the craft or commercially-available inflatable bags or blocks of foam. The extra flotation serves as insurance against loss of life and craft by keeping boats more manageable when swamped or capsized, a distinct advantage over log rafts and skin boats.

Open Canoe

As the original native craft of North America, the open canoe is part of the history of both Canada and the United States. The very word came from a West Indian name for the primitive dugout craft seen by Columbus on his voyage. The canoe has played an important role in the growth of both nations and continues in use for recreation.

Open canoes are the most popular muscle-powered boat in North America.

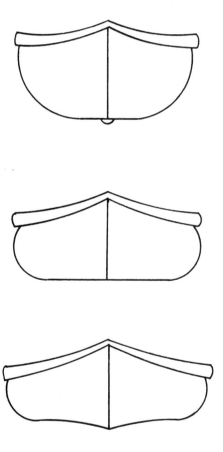

Hull designs

Top: round

Middle: flat

Bottom: V-shape

They are found mostly on mild and moderately turbulent rivers as well as on flat water. Usually a two-person craft, an open canoe is highly versatile, portagable, and lots of fun. It is also fragile and unstable until you learn how to live in it.

What makes a good river canoe is not what makes a good lake canoe. The longer the boat and the less rocker (the convex curve of the bottom), the better it will track (follow a straight line), which is fine if you don't have to dodge rocks. The higher the sides, the bigger waves the craft can manage but also the greater wind resistance it will have. River canoes can afford to have higher sides than lake canoes. Select the one that will best serve your purpose.

River canoes should not have keels. Keels reduce maneuverability and catch on low-water rocks and other obstacles. Stability depends upon the width and how well the load (including people) is balanced. "The real determiner of stability is the shape of a cross-section of the widest point of the canoe," says Harry Roberts, former editor of *Wilderness Camping.*

In other words, hull design is more critical than the width of the craft. In general, the shorter and broader the canoe, the better it will maneuver, but the slower it will be. The longer and narrower canoe is faster but less maneuverable. With proper hull design, you can get the best combination in a

craft — speed, stability, maneuverability, and carrying capacity. No two paddlers seem to agree on which craft has best attained that happy medium.

A great many canoe paddlers today are following the lead of the racers and using cruiser-type craft like the We-no-nah Sundowner which Dick and Mary Lund paddled on our 1980 Namekagon-St. Croix trip. Such craft are ideal for relatively mild rivers but are inappropriate for whitewater beyond Class II. Ann Dwyer, a superb paddler who manufactures river equipment and leads canoe trips in the West, likes cruisers too, but not for serious whitewater. For that, she recommends Sawyer's 17-footer, the 16-foot Whitewater OCA built by Blue Hole, and the 16-foot Mad River Explorer. All of them are made of Royalex.

Royalex is one of the new synthetic materials that has brought about drastic changes in canoe construction during the past decade. Royalex is a vinyl-ABS-foam sandwich (VAFS) material developed by Uniroyal. Oltonar and Sawyerlex are among similar VAFS materials.

But Royalex is only the first of many synthetic materials being used by canoe manufacturers. Some of the more innovative manufacturers are building canoes from several different sophisticated fabrics. Mad River is using Royalex, Kevlar 49, and all-cloth fiberglass. Voyageur Canoe Company in

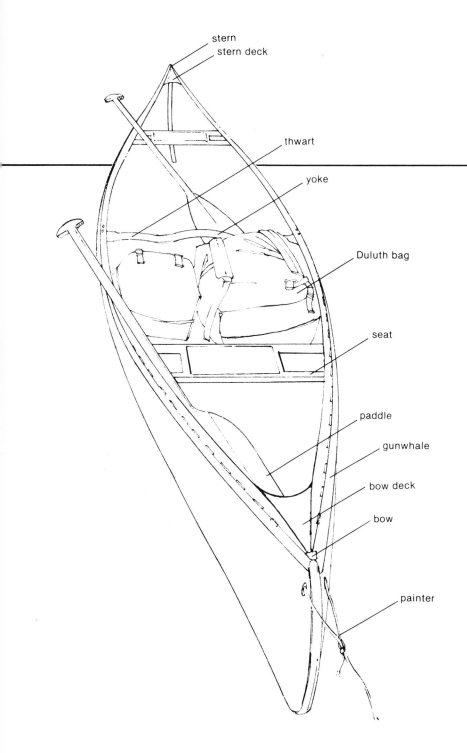

stern
stern deck
thwart
yoke
Duluth bag
seat
paddle
gunwhale
bow deck
bow
painter

Canada uses both Kevlar and fiberglass. Old Town uses fiberglass, polyethylene, Oltonar, wood, and wood-and-canvas.

Canoe prices vary widely and freight costs are high, but you can buy a Coleman canoe, a best-seller because of its low price and tough shell, for under $350. Many aluminum and fiberglass canoes sell for $300 to $600. Oltonar and Royalex canoes go for $400 to $700. Wood-and-canvas boats, because of the labor-intensive production, are more expensive.

Of the four basic materials used for making canoes — wood, aluminum, fiberglass and synthetics — natural materials have given way to the other three for mass-produced craft. Wood-and-canvas canoes and the classically beautiful cedar strippers are still being built. A few individuals and small companies still make birchbark canoes and other high quality hand-crafted boats.

Fiberglass is malleable and can be formed into the best designs for sleek, efficient hulls, but it is not as tough as the newer synthetics. Fiberglass canoes are actually fiberglass-reinforced plastic, easy to repair in the field and flexible enough to endure a lot of trauma on the river.

Aluminum is declining in popularity, but there are a lot of aluminum boats on North American rivers. Depending on the weather, they are either cold or hot, and noisy. They catch on rocks and leave dangerous wreckage when they break. For all these disadvantages, they are relatively inexpensive, durable, and easy to maintain. They come close to being an all-around canoe and are most often used as livery canoes. I own an 18-foot Grumman which can haul a lot of gear. It's part of the family.

Many of the new synthetic materials are expensive, some are extremely lightweight, and most of them take coloring readily. Some deteriorate under ultraviolet light. Synthetics are frequently used in a variety of combinations to take advantage of particular characteristics. A product that is lightweight and tough but deteriorates in sunlight will be covered with or blended with another product that will protect it.

Before you buy a canoe, read the latest edition of *Canoe's* annual buyer's guide. Rent or borrow a canoe. Talk to other paddlers. If I were to buy a canoe today, knowing that my 18-foot Grumman is still functional for many purposes, I would get a small (16- or 17-foot) Royalex whitewater design. If I were to

replace the canoe I have, I might go to a fiberglass cruiser. I would love to own a cedar stripper, but I'm not sure I would use it enough to make it worthwhile.

Canoes may be bought with yokes for carrying them to the river, even if you don't portage. You can also buy yokes and install them yourself, or make them.

Kayak

Kayaks and decked canoes are the ultimate whitewater craft and are the hard-hulled answer to technical rivers. This section might better be headed "Boats You Wear," since both kayaks and decked canoes are form-fitted to the paddler. If you capsize, you roll back to an upright position (if you know how, otherwise you bail out and swim). There are two differences between a kayak and a decked canoe. In the kayak, you sit and use a double-bladed paddle, while in a decked canoe, you kneel and use a single-bladed paddle.

Structurally, they look very similar. They are variously called C-1 (a one-person decked canoe), C-2 (a two-person decked canoe), K-1 (one-person kayak), and K-2 (two-person kayak). A two-person craft has two cockpits. Experience in a C-1 is advisable before taking on a C-2 or a K-2.

While kayaks and decked canoes are being built of new materials such as polyethylene or Royalex, most are still

made of fiberglass reinforced plastic. Most of the new materials are very experimental and I would stick with proven materials and technology until something is demonstrably better.

Perception is the leader in mass-producing plastic boats by the cheaper roto-molding process. In some cases, they are incorporating the new materials into the old. Perception's kayaks are in demand by advanced paddlers because of the price (low) and durability (high).

Another interesting trend in the world of kayaks and decked canoes is away from high-volume (large capacity) boats toward low-volume (small-capacity) boats used in racing. When paddlers go camping, they are more likely to take along a support raft instead of using larger kayaks to carry gear. They can have more fun in the small craft and not worry about carrying capacity. Eric Evans, world class slalom kayaker, says, "A kayak camping trip with raft or canoe support is ideal because you can carry more gear. If worse comes to worst, a kayak will suffice, but use a large touring model if possible."

Longer craft are faster, but harder to turn. Wider craft are more stable.

Dory

Because all kayaks are made to roll, stability is related more to the paddler than to craft design.

Before kayaks and decked canoes are ready for the river, they need to be outfitted with seats (for kayaks), foot braces, knee pads, thigh braces, and knee cups (for decked canoes), back strap (for kayaks), and grab loops. Cockpit rims must also be installed if they are not already in the craft. Pedal-type foot braces are safer than the commonly-used bar braces, which have caused several fatalities when paddlers caught their feet on them and could not bail out of their boats. Grab loops of nylon webbing or rope should be attached to both bow and stern. Seats, braces, and pads should be installed to fit you. After all, you are wearing the craft.

Several folding boats similar to kayaks are also used for river camping, especially in Alaska and Canada and in a few pockets in the continental United States. Commonly a wooden frame covered with a rubberized canvas, these boats take up little space until they are rigged at the river. They require no inflation pump nor are they subject to sudden deflation. More stable than most kayaks but less durable, they can carry enough gear and food for moderately long trips.

Dories give less than rafts but are highly maneuverable. They can be used in heavy whitewater with light loads but are used for fishing trips on many rivers milder than Class IV. The word dory is of American origin, coming from a Central American and West Indian word for the dugout log craft. It has been applied to a small, flat-bottomed, rowed boat commonly used in ocean fishing in many parts of the world. Adopted for river fishing in the Pacific Northwest where it is frequently called a drift boat or McKenzie boat (for Oregon's McKenzie River), the dory may be the most aesthetically pleasing craft on the river today.

Originally made of wood, today the dory is often made of fiberglass or aluminum. Its basic shape is still the same: flat-bottomed with widely-flared sides and heavily-rockered, long axis. It is a deep boat which may be either open with a pair of seats, or decked and compartmentalized. For day fishing trips it is usually left open, but for extended whitewater camping trips, it is normally decked. Dories, with their many watertight compartments, have tremendous carrying capacity and offer extra flotation.

In the past decade, the dory users have expanded their territory to include

much of western Canada and the northern Rockies. I have seen dories on the rivers of California, of southeastern Utah, and even on a few rivers in the eastern United States such as the Kennebec Gorge. Martin Litton uses them for commercial trips in the Grand Canyon and on other western rivers.

These heavily-rockered boats that can turn on the tip of a wave are infinitely maneuverable and operate on the principle that they can avoid the obstacles in rapids that rafts might be stable enough to withstand. They are commonly 14½ feet long (varying from 12 to 20 feet),

with a 4-foot-wide floor flaring out to as much as 7 feet at the oarlocks.

Don Hill, who builds wooden dories, says that the best aluminum dories are made by Alumaweld in southern Oregon, and the best fiberglass dories are made by Labro in Washington.

As for the more traditional wooden boats, no one builds them any better than Don Hill himself. He also sells kits at lower prices than whole boats. Sixty percent complete, the dory kits let you do the time-consuming work and have the pleasure of seeing the craft come to form under your own hands.

Sportyak

The sportyak is the small-is-beautiful answer to river running. Designed as a dinghy and used as such in many corners of the globe, the sportyak came into its own as a river craft in 1963 when Bill Belknap, Otis (Doc) Marston, and a small party of intrepid river runners used the tiny craft for a month-long trip through the Grand Canyon at historically-low water levels. That was the year the Bureau of Reclamation began impounding Colorado River water behind Glen Canyon Dam.

Made from high-density linear polyethylene material bonded together in a clamshell molding process, the sportyak is a plastic bathtub with a double hull in a one-piece rigid structure with floatable foam between the layers. It is durable, attractive, and practical. It floats even when full of water. The double sheet of thermoplastic is vacuum-formed and fused together so an airspace is left between the sheets, providing flotation. It is a hard-hulled inflatable that never needs inflation.

Small (7 feet by 36 inches for the Sportyak II, 8 feet by 45 inches for the Sportyak III) and lightweight (42 pounds and 75 pounds respectively), this craft is virtually indestructible in normal whitewater use. It is rowed from built-in oar mounts using 5- or 6-foot oars in chromium-plated oarlocks. It comes in white and a choice of green, turquoise, or orange and is made by Dayton Marine Products, Inc.

The sportyak is too small to carry enough camping gear for an extended river trip without frequent re-supply stops. The best method is to go sportyakking with a support raft to carry the gear. A small (no more than 3½ h.p.) motor can be used if long stretches of flat water are to be negotiated. It can also be rigged for sailing, but the sportyak is essentially a small rowboat that can survive most whitewater.

Johnboat

The johnboat is a long, narrow craft powered and controlled with paddles or pole(s). It is used for traveling upstream or downstream on mild water. Used mostly in the South, it is native to the streams of the Ozark Mountains in Arkansas and Missouri.

There are small areas in the South where the johnboat was traditionally used, its design varying from family to family and carried down from generation to generation as a closely-guarded secret.

According to Leonard Hall of Caldonia, Missouri, who has poled and paddled Ozark rivers for more than 50 years, the johnboat is still in common use, especially on the Current, the lower Black, the Buffalo, and the White rivers. While many of the old traditional wooden johnboats have disappeared, local fishermen still use the basic design in their aluminum fishing boats. In some

parts of the Ozarks, a paddle made from sassafras wood is traditional.

While most johnboats are shorter (14 to 16 feet long), some may be as much as 24 or even 30 feet long. Level on the bottom for two-thirds of its length, it is turned up at each end (raked), the amount of rise dependent upon family designs. The bow and stern narrow to as little as 12 inches in some designs but are normally nearer to 30 inches. The craft is between one and two feet deep. Many have a double keel.

In the horse-and-wagon days, johnboats were built at the river, used for carrying heavy loads of goods and produce, and then sold for lumber at the market town. While most johnboats are flat-bottomed and square-ended, they have good rocker (degree of upward curve of the hull) for maneuvering and are relatively stable.

Inflatable Raft

Inflatable rafts are much more common in the West than in the East or in Canada, but recent commercial whitewater paddle raft trips have increased their use in several eastern states. Rafting is also increasing in Alaska, the midwestern United States, and parts of Canada where it had been virtually unknown a few years ago.

Rafts (synthetic rubber boats) come in a great range of sizes, materials, designs, and quality. Most of the inflatable rafts are made from neoprene, polyester, urethane, nylon, and Hypalon in a variety of complex combinations. All of them have a base fabric (usually nylon) covered with the synthetic rubber.

In selecting a river-worthy raft, look for a sturdy material in a tough woven fabric (nylon, dacron) covered with one of the time-tested synthetic rubbers (neoprene, Hypalon, polyester). Be sure the craft has several inflation chambers and conveniently-placed screw-type valves that will not fail under impact. D-rings should be appropriately placed and well attached (early made-in-Japan products could be torn off by hand, and plastic D-rings broken from lifting the empty raft). Look for smooth contours and smooth seams, for bow and stern lift, for rigidity when inflated, and for air-holding ability. (Test it overnight.) Before you buy a raft, try it on water to determine its maneuverability, response and feel, and its appearance on the water.

There are a variety of sizes, from small (8 or 9 feet long) dinghy-types to professional river-running models (13 to 22 feet long). The largest are the huge pontoons used in the Grand Canyon, on the Thompson, the upper Snake, and the Missouri. Most of the boats you might consider for serious river running will fall in the 12- to 20-foot range and will cost over $1000.

Maravia Corporation builds its boats of polyvinyl chloride (PVC) fabric in a pattern that minimizes the number of seams. Their boats range from the 12-foot Zephyr and the 12-foot, 4-inch Elan to the 18-foot and 20-foot, 6-inch New River I and II. These boats come in white, blue, and yellow. Rubber Crafters of West Virginia is presently the leading domestic supplier of boats to the commercial river running industry. Its boats are made of black neoprene and nylon and come in a variety of models from 12-foot rafts to 37-foot pontoons.

Avon boats (made in England of Hypalon fabric) and Campways boats (made in Japan of Hypalon) are the two biggest sellers of river boats to commercial outfitters. I own an Avon Professional and a Campways Miwok II—both popular boats. I have used them both on very heavy water. At the moment, I am partial to the Pro.

Rogue Inflatables sells a Hypalon-nylon product made in Taiwan which comes in three models: the Rogue (17 feet, 8 inches); the McKenzie (14 feet, 9 inches); and the Illinois (11 feet, 6 inches). Vladimir Kovalik, who has designed boats for Avon, Campways, and Holcomb (forerunner of Maravia), has recently designed a new family of Hypalon boats made in Italy that includes the Falcon (14 feet), the Eagle (16 feet), and the Condor (17 feet, 6 inches)

to be marketed by Wilderness Equipment.

Northwest River Supplies, a supplier of most of the boats mentioned above, has developed a less expensive craft they call the Sport (15 feet). Campways now markets a less expensive Blue Line series. If you want to buy an inflatable raft, be prepared to spend the money it takes to get the best boat and outfit it properly.

If you plan to paddle the raft, you are all set once you have a good pump and a few appropriately-placed ropes plus the waterproof bags and boxes for carrying what you may need. On the other hand, if you plan to row the raft (and I highly recommend that you consider doing so), you will need a frame for mounting the oars.

Metal frames, usually built of aluminum or steel pipe, are sturdy and less likely to be damaged on the river than wooden frames, but they are more expensive and harder to repair. I have used them and like them a great deal, especially for fly-in trips and other break-apart situations. However, I have always built my own from wood.

Wood is less expensive, heavier, and less sturdy, than the pipe used to build metal frames. Wooden frames are more prominent. They rest on top of the tubes where people may be injured by contact with them, while metal frames are usually nestled into the boat between the tubes. Still, wooden frames are easier to repair on the river. The oar mount is bolted (not nailed or screwed) to the wooden frame.

Whatever frame you use, it is fastened to the craft with nylon ropes, straps, or "hoopie," as they are called by California river runners. It is best to tie or buckle the frame on before the tubes are topped off with air (inflated to proper hardness), which tightens the fit of the frame to the tent.

Frequently frames are augmented with suspended floors attached to the frame or poop decks set on top of the tubes. Floors essentially allow the craft to carry more gear lower, reducing the raft's likelihood of capsizing. Floors should not be so low that a rock beneath the craft could crimp the bottom fabric against the floor, nor so high that ammo boxes don't fit between the floor and the frame. Foam sheets can be placed between the boat bottom and the floor to prevent damage to the bottom. Self-bailing bottoms can be created by punching small holes in the floor flap, protecting the holes from tearing by inserting grommets. Then lash the bottom in so that water can flow back and forth from the river to the inside of the boat. Some craft can be purchased with self-bailing floors. Several companies now offer three-thwart options, which are better for paddle rafting.

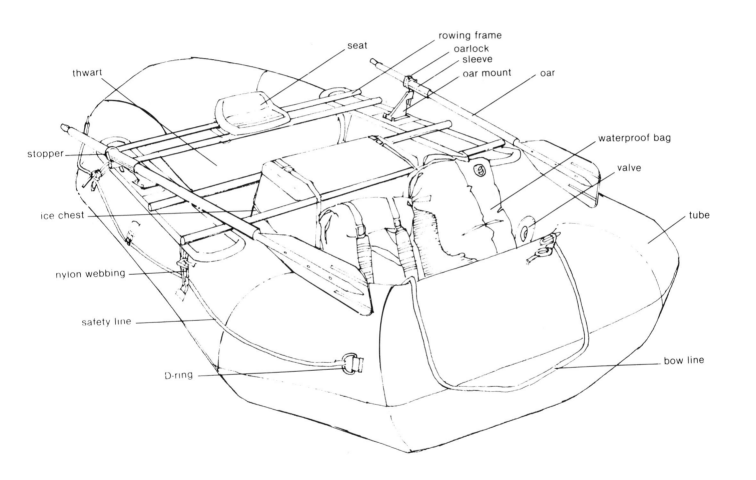

Inflatable Kayak

Inflatable kayaks and canoes — which are really neither kayak nor canoe but rather a hybrid of the two — have become increasingly popular on North American rivers during the past decade. Jerry Bentley of Grants Pass, Oregon, has taught thousands of people on his Orange Torpedo Trips how to paddle their own inflatables. A number of commercial operators offer them as options on other kinds of trips.

Both the inflatable canoes and kayaks function fine in Class III whitewater, but beyond that degree of difficulty, I would not rely on them. They are not big enough to carry much camping gear and are usually supported by rafts on river camping trips. They are lots of fun and good craft to use for learning paddle techniques. I have a Leisure Imports Sea Eagle that I have used occasionally in Hells Canyon, the Main Salmon, and other rivers. Many inflatables are not built to last long and are rather easily punctured.

Most of these craft are built of polyvinyl chloride (PVC). In my opinion, PVC by itself is not river-worthy, but some of the more recent fabrics have included an inner reinforcing fiber bonded to plastic.

Leisure Imports markets the Pyrawa sport canoes (made in France) and the Sea Eagle explorer canoes (made in Italy)

of DynaWeb, a PVC, polyester thread, PVC sandwich. The Sevylor products made in France are marketed as the Tahiti and Tahiti Sport. The Austrian-made Semperit Dolphic II (constructed of 3-ply neoprene, polyester, and Hypalon with three main air chambers) is a sturdier craft but is more expensive. Probably the best inflatable canoe/kayak I have seen is the Metzeler Spezi (or Skate). Made in Austria, it too is constructed from 3-ply neoprene, polyester, and Hypalon and will inflate to be a very rigid craft.

Paddles

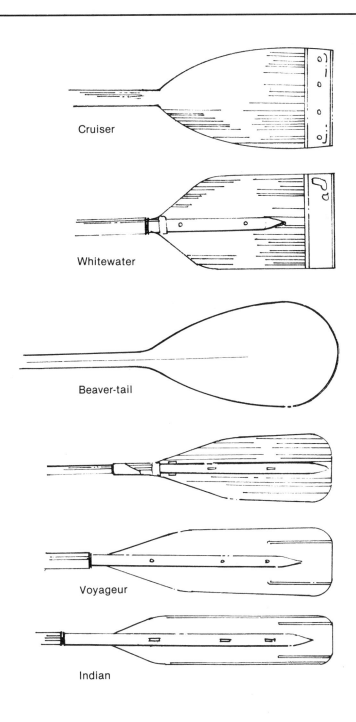

Cruiser

Whitewater

Beaver-tail

Voyageur

Indian

Different craft and different river conditions call for different paddles. Double-bladed paddles are best for kayaks and inflatable canoe/kayaks, and single-bladed paddles are best for canoes and rafts. The paddle will need to be longer for a raft because paddlers sitting on inflated tubes are further from the water. Paddles are still longer for the person doing the steering in a raft.

The simpler wooden paddles are traditional, inexpensive, and widely used. Many modern paddlers have turned to more expensive laminated wood, fiberglass, and plastic models. Paddle blades have many shapes, depending upon their specific use, but there is a general trend toward wider blades. Shallow rivers call for short blades and short paddles.

To find the right paddle for you, try various hand grips (T, pear, flat, Indian) and lengths. Weight and durability are considerations on long trips. (Always carry along a spare.) paddles that are very flexible are inefficient; ones that are too stiff will tire you out quickly.

My wife and I have two paddles each: a Clement laminated wood with an 8-inch blade made in Canada, 60 inches long for me (I am 5 feet, 9 inches tall) and 56 inches long for my wife (she's 5 feet, 2

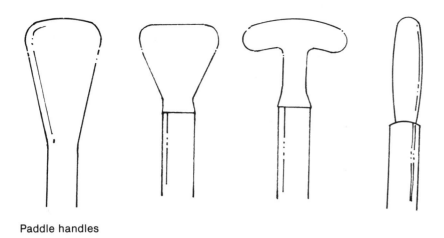

Paddle handles

Oars

inches tall); and a pair of Mohawks with aluminum shafts and ABS plastic blades in the same lengths. We use the Mohawks for shallow or rough rivers, the wooden ones for lakes and gentle rivers. The wooden paddles are not protected with fiberglass but should be. They are beginning to show wear after seven years of use.

As a spare, I carry a Carlisle paddle, 60 inches long, with a T-grip and an ABS blade — a paddle I found in Westwater Canyon. It is stiffer than I like for long-term paddling, but I know I can depend upon it.

Traditionally, paddles have been measured to the chin or the armpit of the paddler. The current trend is toward shorter paddles and more frequent strokes. If you sit on the seat, your paddle should be slightly longer than if you kneel most of the time. A current practice is to take your normal paddling position, kneeling or sitting, place the paddle upside down (grip on the floor), and grab the shaft with the off-hand (opposite side) where it joins the blade. The proper length has the arm parallel to the floor at a point between the chin and the nose.

Metal, fiberglass, and ABS paddles need little care. Wooden blades are often tipped with fiberglass or are copperplated to protect them from damage. They should be oiled or varnished to protect them from water damage.

Oars are used to power and control dories, rafts, and sportyaks. They are attached to the craft by means of oarlocks which cradle the oars. Oarlocks are built into the craft or into a frame attached to the craft.

At least four types of oarlock arrangements are used: oar horns, rings, clamp-ons, and thole-pins. The oar horns are the traditional rowboat Y into which the oar nestles. Rowers use two methods, one with fixed oars, the other with feathering oars. Fixed oars have a pin placed through the shaft of the oar at the appropriate fulcrum point or a pair of metal plates bolted around the oar shaft. The feathering oar makes use of a stopper of some sort to keep the oar from going beyond a certain point outboard. The latter arrangement is also used with ring-type oarlocks.

The clamp-on oarlocks fit the diameter of the oar shaft and have the advantage of not weakening the oar with a bolt through the shaft. However, like the oar horn and pin system, the oar cannot be feathered because it is fixed. Oars are usually wrapped with nylon rope or have some other tough material glued to the shaft to reduce wear and tear from oarlock friction.

The thole-pin is a stationary, vertical shaft that is part of the oar mount on a raft frame. The oar is attached to the thole-pin either with a strap (leather,

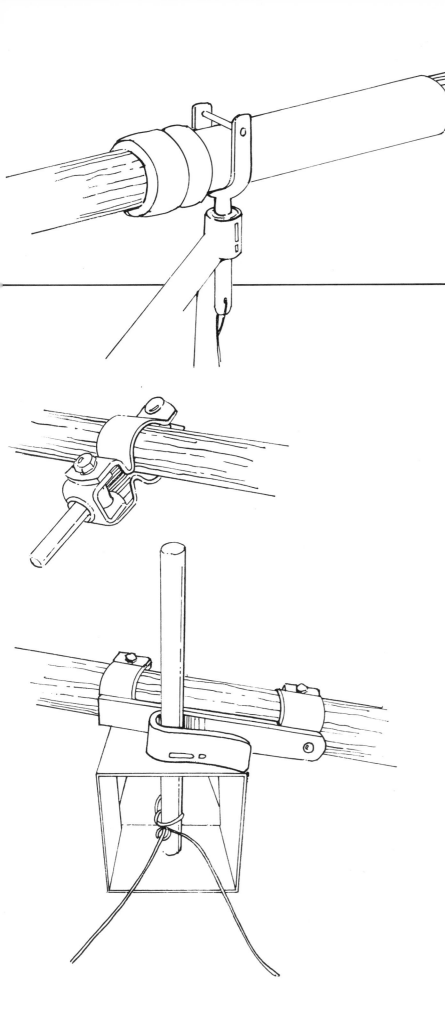

nylon, or conveyer belt) or with a metal clip (California clip). The strap or clip is attached to the oar. U-bolts can be used effectively without weakening the shaft. I use traditional oarlocks with a stopper and my oars can be feathered as well as pulled into the craft to run narrow chutes.

Oar mounts themselves are made of blocks of hardwood or of metal. They can be welded or bolted to metal frames and bolted (not screwed) to wooden ones. Screws may work loose or rip out under stress. Be sure to pad the head of the bolt beneath the frame to reduce wear on the craft fabric.

Wooden oars are traditional, but space-age materials have moved into the market with fiberglass and plastic products that are resilient, lightweight, and strong.

Oars should be roughly two-thirds the length of the craft they are intended to control: 5 feet for a 7-foot sportyak; 11 feet for a 16-foot raft; and 9 to 10 feet for a 14½-foot dory. Some boaters buy longer oars for bigger, stronger shafts and cut them down to size.

A special word about Carlisle plastic oars, which I use. They are developed to take a beating and last. The oars have an aluminum core shaft and are covered with colorful plastic. Blades have "STM" to protect them from ultraviolet deterioration.

Many river runners prefer to stick with tradition, using wooden oars and keeping plastics and colorful equipment out of the backcountry for aesthetic reasons. Carlisle oars do not offend me. They match the bumper strips on my Avon Professional, and they have given me good service.

Sweeps

Sweeps have been used since the 17th century for running North American rivers. They come in numerous patterns and designs, none of which are readily available to my knowledge. They are built as the need dictates. Sweeps consist of a blade attached to a long, curved or bent handle connected to a fulcrum mounted on the craft.

The common sweep mount is similar to an oar mount. A metal tripod or a block of wood has a hole lined with a bushing to absorb friction wear. The sweep handle, made of hollow pipe or wood, is attached to an oarlock which fits into the matched hole in the mount. The oarlock attachment may be made with a pin through the sweep handle and the horns of the oarlock, or with a clasp around the handle. Some use the clip arrangement common on inflatable raft rigs.

The long handle is curved so that the blade will reach the water at an effective angle. The blade is designed to get the most out of its surface contact with the water. In shallow rivers, the blade may be long and narrow, while in deeper rivers, it may be short and wide. Blades are constructed of a combination of metal, fiberglass, or wood. A common sweep is a metal pole with a plywood blade wrapped in fiberglass bolted onto the pole.

Sweeps designed for a single

Poles

Poles for poling canoes and johnboats can be cut in the woods in an emergency, but most polers now use aluminum poles.

Poles are 10 to 14 feet long, depending upon the river and personal preferences. Wooden poles should be peeled of their bark and smoothed to reduce wear and tear on hands. Pole ends can be tipped with duckbill shoes of galvanized iron which open with downward pressure to form a bearing surface but close when drawn upward. Metal (aluminum is good) gripping shoes are also available.

Gigs, small trident forks for spearing fish or frogs, may be used as ends. In areas with muddy bottoms, you can rig your own mudguard to prevent getting stuck. Commercial mudguards are available, but poling is such a specialized sport that they may be hard to find. Ski-pole baskets are another possibility. Carlisle Paddles, Inc. has recently developed a pole in ABS plastic that takes either a heavy rubber crutch-type tip or a duckbill tip for soft bottoms.

The best source I know for equipment and information on poling is the Mackenzie River Company in St. Louis. Operated by the Beletz brothers (Al, Syl, and Frank) who are among the most ardent polers in North America, this Midwest establishment also carries *Canoe Poling,* the sport's best source book.

operator are longer and balanced with counterweights to make them easier to handle. To do this, molten lead is poured into the hollow pipe, or sheet lead is wrapped around the pipe at an appropriate place and fixed with radiator hose clamps. Where river bottoms are of highly abrasive materials, it pays to use metal blades or to cover wooden blades with fiberglass to protect them.

GEAR

The pile of gear that grew at the take-out on our mid-summer Salmon River/Hells Canyon expedition was amazing. Several parties ended their trips that day, and they just kept coming, landing, and unloading gear onto the rocky beach. There were folding cots and tables from the commercial party, wooden floors and frames, flabby deflated rafts, metal ammo cans, colorful ice chests and water jugs, ABS paddles and oars, bright orange life jackets, waterproof gear bags, rubber bungies, nylon ropes and tarps and safety lines, wooden kitchen boxes, chemical toilet gear. It was an unbelievable conglomeration of paraphernalia.

It was nice to have the extra oars and the large tarp, but we'd used them only for rigging a sauna. The extra ice chest had kept us in ice and cold beer for most of the trip. The life jackets had not been needed to save anyone's life, but they had been worn and used to swim a few of the minor rapids. The mirror had been used for shaving and for pointing out the deer on the ridge. The waterproof bags had kept our clothes and sleeping bags dry. Days had been long and the water fast enough that we did not need the lanterns at night, but we'd had them along just in case.

A decade ago most river running equipment was spin-off gear from military surplus or other outdoor activities. Waterproof containers and kitchen boxes were built in home workshops. So were many boats. People improvised—they made do with homemade gear and less-than-professional equipment.

Much of that has changed. River running activities all over the continent have become so popular that whole new industries have sprung up virtually overnight. The development and testing of new equipment continues, and new products emerge every season, take an area by storm, then fade into the background as better products emerge elsewhere. Some products work; some don't. Variations are made. And prices rise with the quality of gear.

But you don't necessarily need all the new-fangled inventions if you have the basics that have been used since Lewis and Clark: food, fire, clothing, and shelter. Of course, the members of the Lewis and Clark expedition were not always warm, safe, and comfortable. They did a lot of improvising. Lt. Doane's men, on the other hand, some seventy years later, had for shelter "an Indian lodge . . . constructed of army wagon covers cut in proper form and fourteen feet in diameter. This weighed but thirty pounds and sheltered the entire party (seven men)."

That cross between an Indian tipi and a military accouterment lasted throughout the Doane party's late-fall exploration of the upper Snake. They also had "buffalo coats and moccasins, rubber boots (later lost in an upset in the Snake River Canyon near Alpine Junction) and overshoes, heavy underclothing and plenty of robes and blankets." Their kitchen gear consisted of "two fry pans, two Dutch ovens, four camp kettles and some mess pans." What more could you want?

Safety

Aside from common sense, the most important piece of safety equipment on the river is the personal flotation device, or PFD, also called a life jacket. It can only save your life if you wear it, wear it properly, and have the right size. In study after study of drowning associated with river running, it has been found that a large majority of the victims either were not wearing a PFD, or were not wearing it properly.

The U.S. Coast Guard requires that you have a PFD along for every person in the craft. As long as you are carrying it, you might as well wear it. It might save your life. The Coast Guard identifies five types of PFDs: Type I—life jacket; Type II—buoyant vest; Type III—buoyant device; Type IV—throwable device; and Type V—special devices.

Type I PFDs are the best for heavy whitewater, but they are bulky and uncomfortable. They use airtight packets of flotation material that are sewn into

pockets in the jacket. When ruptured, these packets make the PFD worse than useless because they then soak up water and weight the wearer down. If you sit, kneel, lie or stand on, or use for padding a Type I PFD, you may have a death trap on your body.

Many kayakers and canoeists prefer a Type III buoyant device made especially for whitewater paddlers. The best way to select a PFD is to try several until you find one that fits well and will support you. Test it in the water before you need it, and wear it on the river. The person who doesn't wear one is the person who drowns. Take good care of it, and it will take good care of you.

Helmets are worn by virtually all decked boat paddlers to protect their heads when they roll. More and more whitewater canoeists and rafters are wearing them. Sometimes local governmental ordinances require helmets. Everything from hockey to motorcycle helmets have been worn, but whitewater helmets that offer a good compromise between weight, drainage, and shock

Personal Emergency Kit

knife (Swiss Army)
fishhook and line
matches in waterproof container
high-energy food (small amount)
space blanket
watch
whistle
mirror

Party Emergency Gear

map of area   duct tape
flashlight   saw
lots of rope   ax
sleeping bag   tinder
medical kit (see First Aid)
repair kit (see below)
tarp for shelter
hand winch or block and tackle
chemical fire starter
carabiners

Wilderness Emergency

compass   fishing gear
radio   gun
signalling equipment (flare guns,
Strobolite)
extra food rations

Repair Kit

punches   emory cloth
awls   sandpaper
drills   scissors
rasp   saws (wood, metal)
pliers   vice-grip pliers
wrenches   screw drivers
screws   extra D-rings
nuts, bolts   extra valves
appropriate solvents, thinners
appropriate cements, glues
patching material
containers for mixing
heavy-duty needle
heavy thread (dental floss)
check list and pencil
spare parts for pumps, stoves
extra webbing, rope, straps
buffing tools

---

protection are now available.

Wet suits are highly desirable in cold weather and cold water. During the mild winters of the Pacific Northwest, where I live, we wear wet suits in whitewater from October through June. The lighter weight suits (1/8- and 3/16-inch) in mid-thigh and short-sleeved cuts are good for warm-weather, cold-water situations, but full hoods and gloves are best for winter trips.

Wet boots are great for cold-water trips. They help to preserve body heat and offer protection against rocks and other sharp objects. The best wet boots are ones with heavy fabric soles. No matter what the weather, you should always wear some type of shoes. Bare feet often get cut, scraped, and sunburned.

Ropes on the boat, both bow and stern lines, and "chicken" lines (to hold onto going through rapids and turbulent water) are important safety equipment. I believe every group should carry a throw line per boat.

You can not be totally safe. Part of the wilderness experience is the possibility of getting lost and finding your way out. In your search for total solitude, part of the price you pay is the real possibility that you will be completely on your own with no one to bail you out. As Colin Fletcher says, "Visitors should pay in the coin of the realm."

Certain items of emergency gear should be carried with you at all times (in your pockets, strapped to your belt, sewn into your PFD, or in a fanny pack). Other items should be carried with the party on any trip, but for real wilderness situations you may want additional items.

Waterproof Containers

You will sleep better if you keep your sleeping bag dry, eat better if you keep the river out of the oatmeal, and enjoy the trip more if your extra socks are dry at the end of the day. Good waterproof containers help guarantee dry gear. Many river runners use the double plastic bag routine and tie everything first in

separate plastic bags to guard against wetting. If you have the proper containers, however, you can avoid that.

If you are going to spend any real time on the rivers, you might as well go prepared. Military surplus ammunition cans, delousing bags, gas mask bags, and assorted other containers make good river boxes and bags. In fact, many manufacturers who cater to river runners now imitate military surplus gear at a higher price (and usually higher quality).

You can also use ice chests and water coolers to store and carry gear you want to keep dry on the river, but it doesn't cost much to go first class and get some real river equipment like the Dragonfly Design river bags (tough nylon shells with heavy-duty plastic liners) or Voyageur's Camp-Pak bags, which are a pain to close but keep things dry as long as the inner plastic bag remains sound. (I have had a couple go out at the seams.) Northwest River Supplies makes a series of heavy-duty Hypalon duffle-type bags.

For gear that needs protection from impact as well as water, ammo cans are best, even though they may be too heavy for kayaks and canoes. I have successfully used the plastic Sport Safe of Recreation Creations, Inc. and the Pelican Products' Equipment case. The Pelican case is awkward in a canoe, but it works fine on my raft. The Sport Safe is ideal for the stern position in my canoe because it opens on the side.

Ammo boxes are standard food containers for raft trips. If you use small ammo boxes for cameras, be sure to check the waterproof seal and replace it if it is faulty. Pad the insides with foam to protect the camera. Ammo boxes also make good containers for first aid kits, repair kits, and spices. Use carabiners to fasten them down.

Food for kayak/decked canoe trips can be carried in small plastic bags or river bags designed for enclosed paddle craft. For canoe trips, Adirondack baskets and Duluth packs—both of which can be portaged easily—are popular. I prefer those from Dragonfly Designs because they have straps, can be portaged with ease, and are waterproof.

Duluth packs are large canvas bags that come in a variety of sizes and buckle down with straps over the top. They have backpack straps and a tumpline which can be fitted over the forehead to distribute the load on a portage. Adirondack baskets are patterned after early American Indian baskets used for carrying food and gear. They can be carried like a backpack, but if you expect water to get into the canoe, either from rain or splashes from the river, make or buy a rain cover for them.

Maps are important on river trips and need to be handy. Map cases are available at many outdoor equipment stores and river running shops, but you can make serviceable waterproof map cases from clear plastic sheets joined at the edges with duct tape.

Fire

Fire gear is not necessary if you don't plan to build an open fire and do plan to do all your cooking on a stove. If you build a fire in heavy-use areas, you should carry a fire pan (a metal plate with raised edges to contain the fire). You then carry out or bury the ashes and charcoal. A fire pan raised on legs can serve as a camp stove and be a very effective garbage burner as well.

If you use a campfire for cooking and heating water, you should have a folding grill so that you do not have to build a fire pit. Your grill should fit your fire. A grill is good for drying garbage to be burned, as well as supporting griddles, pots, and pans.

Cooking

Cooking equipment need not be elaborate, but it should be adequate. If you don't cook on an open fire, you need a camp stove. Small backpacker models are ideal for unsupported kayak trips and small parties. For larger groups, you will need two- and three-burner stoves or several smaller ones.

David Sumner, an outdoorsman with whom I have done fair bit of river camping, tested nearly forty stoves for *Backpacker* magazine a few years ago and found that the Mountain Safety Research (MSR) gas model was best. He uses it on all his river trips. I use an old reliable Svea that I received as a gift in 1961. Coleman's Peak I also works well. The Swiss-made Sigg cook kit is an ideal set of pots and pans for small groups, especially if you combine two or three sets from different party members.

I had used a Coleman two-burner for years until a friend took it to Alaska for a Tatshenshini trip and somehow blew it up. (Luckily, no one was hurt.) I have replaced it with another Coleman two-burner for raft trips and with a propane two-burner for canoe trips. If you use petro-fuel stoves, you need to carry along extra fuel and funnels for recharging stoves.

As pots, pans, and other cooking containers, nesting aluminum sets are lightweight and compact. Dutch ovens and griddles made of aluminum are available, but I have always used the traditional cast-iron ones. For cooking, you will also need large knives, forks, spoons, can openers, ladles, pancake turners, peelers, graters, whisks, and plastic containers for mixing dried milk and pancake batter.

Other equipment for the fire includes an ax, hatchet, saw, and pair of pliers, as well as a pair of heavy gloves for handling hot items on the grill. Gloves are handy for keeping yourself clean when handling blackened pots. A special bag or box should be used for storing the blackened gear and utensils to keep them from getting everything else covered with soot. A pair of tongs may be handy to have around the fire for moving coals, steaks on the grill, and for Dutch oven cooking.

Roger Drayna, a Wisconsin paddler and old friend, uses a short chain to plop into the plastic container to help mix milk and batters. Don't take anything along that you won't use or need. What you do take depends upon how elaborately you eat, how much you have to portage, and how long you will be on the river.

For dishwashing, have enough large pots. Heat water in metal containers, then pour it into large, plastic containers for the dishwashing. People can bring their own cups, plates, and utensils for eating. Ice chests, coolers, and water jugs are essential parts of river trips if you plan to eat and drink well.

Shelter

Tents for shelter and privacy are carried on most river trips. In northern climes, they are essential for protection against the hoards of black flies and mosquitoes.

A very practical tent is the dome. The dome does not need to be anchored with tent pegs but may be (and should be when left alone). I saw a family lose one to a gust of wind in Ruby Canyon on the Colorado River. David Sumner tells of losing one to a clear-air-cell storm on the Green River in Flaming Gorge: "I did not stake the tent. I was well away when the clear-air-cell hit, and actually, it was quite beautiful, but when I got back to camp, the tent was gone. I couldn't find it anywhere within a quarter-mile radius." He searched for three hours, and gave it up for lost. Rangers found it two weeks later, 300 vertical feet and a half-mile away.

I like dome tents but have never owned one myself. I use Coleman's Peak I 4-man when I take my family, and a North Face Tuolumne when I am by myself. If you plan to set up a tent on sand, use extra long tent pegs or anchor all pegs with large rocks.

Tarp tents used for protecting kitchen areas, for sleeping shelters, or for screening toilet areas can be rigged with tarps, ropes, and poles. It reduces the impact on local vegetation to bring your own poles, either aluminum or plastic, but in areas of abundant wood, it may not be as critical.

On our Namekagon-St. Croix canoe trip in the fall of 1980, Dick Lund brought along a 20-feet long, 12-feet wide tarp that we set up to protect camp gear and to shelter the cooking area. We draped it over a rope stretched between two trees, anchored one end to the ground with rope and tent pegs, and flared the other end out with ropes tied to distant trees. To further enhance the head room, we set up a piece of our firewood about eight feet long with a tin can protector on top to lift the center of the fly.

To sleep comfortably, you need very little on most river trips: a ground cloth to keep the moisture in the earth and a light sleeping bag that is kept dry by a good waterproof bag. I usually use an ensolite pad, which also serves to protect the plastic liner of my pack from the sharp surfaces of other gear.

Self-inflating air mattresses (Thermo-a-Rests) seem very useful. Made of lightweight open-cell foam, they expand by themselves when the valve is open and hold air overnight when it is closed. Merely open the valve to deflate it, forcing the air out as you roll it up. I make my own pillow on the spot, filling a stuff bag with a sweater or down vest.

Sleeping bags should be appropriate for the climate. I used a ten dollar cheapy on my first Grand Canyon trip in June and was comfortable. On a late-March trip, I was almost cold in a heavy down bag. I now use a Gerry down bag for all my trips, adjusting the bag and what I wear to the climate. Down is worthless when wet, which is why I don't let my bag get wet. New fiber-filled bags of closed-cell material may be more useful for river trips.

Eric Evans, on his American Sportsman trip for ABC-TV to southern Mexico to run the Rio Jata Te, discovered a new way to sleep: "I found that a nylon, lightweight, fish-net type hammock was a super buy. It was light and easy to pack and made a sleeping bag, pad, and tent superfluous. A poncho or rain suit thrown over you in the rain did the trick." Sounds great, but be sure your river has trees to tie it to.

Clothing

Clothes don't make the man or woman on a river trip, but they go a long way toward keeping him or her warm and comfortable. River clothes are essentially the same for both men and women. They should be comfortable, adequate, and appropriate. There are two philosophies of dressing for river trips: either wear as little as you can get away with, or dress to the teeth to try to stay dry. I err on the side of the unclothed, figuring that it is virtually impossible to stay completely dry.

On any whitewater river, you are going to get wet. Accept that and dress accordingly. In cold weather, a wet suit may be the best attire, but a heavy, full wet suit can be oppressive on a sunny day. You can get by with a lighweight partial wet suit. Layers don't help if you are wet, unless the layers are wool and one of the layers is a windbreaker that will reduce heat loss.

Let's start at the top. A hat is important to keep the sun out of the eyes, to

keep the head warm, and to serve as protection. In areas where insects are a major problem, a hat is needed for attaching a net. Wool stocking caps are great in cold weather. Any number of wide-brimmed, floppy hats will do for the warmer months. If a helmet is appropriate, that may be all you need. In cold weather, you can fit helmets with wool liners to make them warmer. I wear a pixy ski cap in winter, and in the summer, either a baseball cap or a Stetson Derringer that has seen better days. I use a tie cord to keep the hat on in the wind.

Sunglasses are good to have along because the water reflects sunlight into the eyes and under the hat brim. Tie them on and bring along an extra pair in case you lose or break a pair.

For the upper body, wear a tank top or net T-shirt that will dry quickly. Women can wear a swimsuit top under the net shirt. T-shirts and other cotton, short-sleeved shirts are fine for warm days. Synthetic fabrics tend to dry more quickly. Wear long sleeves if you burn and turtlenecks underneath wool if you are as sensitive to wool as I am. For colder weather or evenings in camp, add a wool sweater or a down jacket (if you can keep it dry). Paddle jackets are a must for decked-boat paddlers.

Below the waist, take a swimsuit, a pair of shorts or cut-offs, long pants (if you burn), long johns in cooler weather, a wet suit for wet trips, and a sweat suit for around camp should it get chilly in the evening. Take along an extra pair of everything in case you get wet, as you certainly will on heavy whitewater trips. Kayakers and decked canoe paddlers invariably wear wet suits on the river but should have dry, comfortable clothes for off-river time.

For the feet, wear something. Don't go barefooted. Tennis shoes, sneakers, or running shoes are fine unless they have slipper soles. I like wet boots if the water or the weather is cold. Many river runners in the Midwest, East, and in Canada wear "pacs," which are the rubber-bottom boots with high canvas or

leather tops. In whitewater, these can be dangerous. They can weigh a person down in the water and are much more likely to be caught between rocks. Once the wearer is trapped, he cannot escape because the boot is tied on. Many Southeastern river runners have gone to the plastic strap sandals popularized by the Nantahala Outdoor Center in Bryson City, North Carolina. I always take along a pair of boots for off-river hiking or climbing.

I have never worn gloves on the river except against the cold on midwinter trips. Then I use wool liners in leather gloves or wear down mittens when I don't intend to get wet. When I know I'm going to get wet, I go to Pogies (nylon glove-like garments which cover both hands and paddle shaft) or wet suit gloves or mittens. Leather gloves are handy around the kitchen for picking up hot things.

You can wash underwear, so there is no need to take along a week's supply. Handkerchiefs are handy to keep the sun off the neck, to tie up cuts, and to create a corner-tied cap. I always take along a couple of large bandannas.

You can go light, but be prepared. I often find that I wear about 20% of what I take along 80% of the time, but the rest of the time, I am grateful that I have the other 80% along. Rain gear, wet suits, down vests, and hiking boots take up space and are of little use but are vital when needed.

Rain Gear

I live in the Pacific Northwest where it rains a lot, and I run rivers every month of the year. I appreciate good rain gear, and until recently, I haven't been entirely satisfied with what I had — a hodgepodge of ponchos, plastic parkas, and rubberized granny gowns. I spent a lot of time on the river wishing I had something that really worked. I wore a lot of wool and did some research. I now have a North Face second-generation Gore-Tex rain suit that works.

A lot of people have been unhappy with Gore-Tex. There is Gore-Tex and there is Gore-Tex, and what different manufacturers do with it means a lot.

The Teflon-like material is supposed to breathe, to stop wind and rain from coming in, and to allow perspiration to wick away. Sometimes it works and sometimes it doesn't. My North Face rain suit does. It is expensive, but staying dry on the river is well worth the investment for me.

Avoid ponchos. They whip around in the rain and can be dangerous. They have caused capsizes and drownings. Any loose-fitting rain gear may get in the way. Rain gear should fit, and it should not snag, rip, or tear. Foul-weather gear and sailing gear may be appropriate for river running in some areas at some seasons. Don't stay away from the rivers because of a little rain. Just prepare for it and enjoy it. It is one of the best ways I know to avoid crowds.

Housekeeping

If you head for the river to get away from housekeeping chores, don't let this section throw you. Housekeeping on the river has to do with keeping the craft in livable condition and doing the same in camp. It's no big deal, but it is important to take care of equipment and health for comfort and pleasure on river camping trips.

Inflating crafts have to be filled with air. Hand and foot pumps are normally used for the chore. I personally prefer the J&J pumps sold by most river equipment stores as they can be repaired easily. My 12-year-old nephew kept mine functional for a year and taught me how to care for it when he moved to another part of the country. Avon foot pumps are fast and easy but wear rather poorly and are difficult to patch. Carry at least one pump along for replacing air bleed-off during the heat of the day and for re-inflating the craft if you need to repair one of the air chambers.

Bailing buckets are a necessity on some of the big-water rivers like the New River, the Thompson, and the Colorado, where a single wave can fill a raft with a ton of water. Most canoeists use cut-off bleach bottles (plastic) as a minimal bailing bucket. In heavy whitewater, I like to use 2½-gallon metal pails that can also serve as dishwater and sauna buckets in camp. Large plastic buckets are also good.

Deck covers are used to keep water out of open canoes, but they can also trap the paddlers in a capsized craft. In effect, a spray cover converts the open canoe into a decked canoe without the capacity to roll back to an upright position. Many experienced paddlers are dead set against the use of deck covers because they encourage paddlers to get into water that may be beyond their ability or the capacity of their craft. If the deck cover is used as a spray deck to keep out wind-blown water and the tops of waves, it may be appropriate.

Spray covers for kayakers and decked canoe paddlers are another story. They are part of the standard gear that is used in the sport and are also known as spray skirts because they are worn like a skirt. The lower edge fits over the cockpit rim to provide a water-tight seal from waist to craft. In effect, the paddlers actually wear the craft. The skirt is normally made of nylon or neoprene, the latter probably the better material. The elastic band must fit the cockpit just right—too loose and it lets water in, too tight and it is difficult to free if the paddler has to swim.

Almost all professional river runners and a great many amateurs wear a pair of pliers and a knife on their belts. Both tools come in handy on the river and in camp. The knife can be used to cut an inflatable that is trapping a person, or a rope that is endangering someone's life. More likely, it will be used to cut salami, clean a fish, or split kindling. The pliers have numerous uses, from repair work to pouring hot coffee, from untying stubborn knots to can-opening.

A Swiss Army knife is a handy tool to have on a river trip. Deluxe models have everything from saws and scissors to corkscrews and can-openers. I find a fanny pack very useful. As my body protects it from direct splashes and my rain jacket fits over it, it remains fairly dry, unless I go into the water. Consequently, I carry all kinds of goodies in it — my fix of hard candy and granola bars, my Swiss Army knife, police whistle, and Kleenex packets. I also carry my knife-fork-spoon set, a notebook, pen, roll of film, and any medication I may use during the day for chapped lips or cold sores.

Paul Whithington, who was on the Namekagon-St. Croix trip, takes along absolutely everything you can imagine. He had a whisk broom and dust pan for sweeping sand out of the tent, a sewing kit, signal devices, and a set of flags representing every state, province,

and country in which he has paddled. He doesn't travel all that heavy. He and a partner can portage the whole lot in two trips.

Toiletries, medication, feminine hygiene products, glasses and sunglasses, biodegradable soap, face cloth, toothpaste and dental floss, spare false teeth and Alka-Seltzer, insect repellent and suntan lotion, brush and comb, Chapstick and car keys, wallet and compass, map and guide book, camera and binoculars, fishing gear, and flashlight are all items you may want to take. Some Alaskan and Canadian voyageurs carry shotguns for bears.

Lanterns and flashlights are good to have along for evening use and for exploring riverside caves and old mines. Some parties enjoy more formal recreational activities on the river and take along volleyball nets and balls, horseshoes, Frisbees and chess sets, and books to read during free time.

Whatever you plan to carry along on the river trip in the way of personal and party gear and equipment needs to fit in somewhere. Plan carefully and leave at home the unnecessary things. Take what you need, but need what you take as well.

TECHNIQUE

Moving water is fascinating, fluid, alive. Sit on the bank of a free-flowing river and watch it move, undulate, eddy, swirl, ripple, and explode. It is powerful and dynamic, at times even terrifying. It is musical, methodical, and mysterious. Yet it follows definite laws of physics and flows in predictable patterns.

If you would venture onto its surface, water bears studying. Get to know the river with an intimacy that shows understanding, even love, and a little healthy fear. To run a river successfully and enjoyably, you need to know why moving water does what it does.

It is a challenge to learn to read water and to know its secrets. The skills and techniques you pick up will enable you to negotiate the river on its terms. A few basic principles hold true for all craft.

A craft will move away from the direction in which the water is moved. Push the water backward, and the craft goes forward. Push the water left, the boat goes right. Powerful current requires powerful strokes. Since the river is more powerful than you are, you need to learn to go with the current, to use it to your advantage. Most novice river runners work a lot harder than they have to because they lack experience in reading water and in responding to its subtle messages.

On my first run through the Grand Canyon of the Colorado, I wore myself out at the oars every time Don Neff gave me a turn. I rowed back and forth across the current, fighting eddies and trying to find the main current. On my first Middle Fork (of the Salmon) run in 1972 with Earl Perry, I learned more about technique than I had in more than a dozen years on the upper Snake. Earl knew how to play with the currents that had previously terrified me.

This chapter is about hand-powered methods of control with paddles, oars, sweeps, and poles. While many of the craft discussed here are occasionally operated with outboard motors, motors overpower the river, battling the current rather than using it.

Motors make noise. I like to hear the sound of the canyon wren and of the river itself. Motors create fumes, and the fuel smells less than pleasant. I like to smell beaver castor and wood smoke and the river itself. The blue smoke of motors lies heavily over the river, obliterating the view, distorting it. I like to leave that smoke in the cities and along the highways, not take it into the wilderness.

Just as you know your bicycle—its balance, speed, and response—so you must know your craft on the water. You do not learn this kind of thing on your river camping trip. You must know it before you launch. Certainly, you will learn more as your trip progresses, but you need to know how to control your craft before you ever shove off. This is experience you can gain in a swimming pool, on a lake, or on short trips on mild water. The craft, the means of control, and the river runner must come together in a meaningful way. That marriage is not made in heaven. It comes with research, practice, and experience.

Reading Water

Just as reading is one of the first education skills learned in school, so reading water is one of the most fundamental skills for the river runner to acquire. You cannot respond appropriately to the subtle nuances of a river's current until you can read them and understand their meaning.

Rivers change constantly, cutting in one place, depositing the eroded material in another. Water runs against a bluff, churns back on itself, and undercuts the rock wall, creating a dangerous trap. Sandbars are laid down wherever water slows enough to lose its carrying power. The limbs of fallen trees collect surface flotsam. Islands are built by the river where sandbars catch trees. All these natural obstacles affect the flow of the current.

The surface of the river offers clues to what lies beneath the surface. It will tell you where a rock lies hidden, where the lateral currents flow, and where the main force of the river goes.

Moving water constantly attempts to reach a dynamic equilibrium, an equaling of the forces that cause it to flow. It piles up above obstacles, leaves telltale turbulence on its surface from underwater objects, and forms depressions (holes) and stationary waves (haystacks). Certain combinations of obstructions cause sharp, sometimes deep holes with curl-back waves known as stoppers, souse holes, or hydraulics (though this latter term might be applied to any of the forms created by the dynamics of moving water).

It may seem childish to sit on the bank of a river throwing pieces of wood into the current to see what they do, or rather, what the river does to them. You can discover where it takes them, how the speed of the current varies, and how lateral currents sometimes dominate and alter direction. Such child's play can teach you a great deal about reading water, and even professional river guides and expert kayakers resort to this practice.

When you are in a craft floating on the surface of a river, watch what happens to the water that goes by beneath you. A V pointing upstream indicates some obstacle, while a smooth V that points downstream suggests a clear route to follow. A line of white water indicates a hole, often created by an obstacle you cannot see.

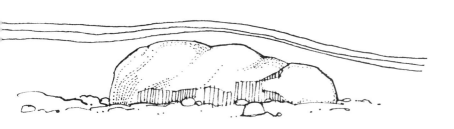

You will discover that barely submerged flat rocks create sleepers with a slight pillow of water bulging above the surface. If the pillow is shallow or your craft has a deep draft, you may ground on a rock. You will discover eddies (reverse currents), which are sometimes big, slow whirlpools but often are violent sucking vortices.

Nothing works quite right until you learn to read water, but once you do, it all starts to come together. You don't learn to read water in one quick, easy lesson any more than you learn to read words that way. It takes lots of practice in different situations. It takes a few mistakes and perhaps a few wettings. Reading water requires sight and hearing. You'd be surprised how much the sound of water flowing over shoals can tell you. It also requires smell. You can actually smell the turbulence of some rapids as the violent current churns up the bottom.

I have run rivers at night, occasionally because of some time-consuming mishap but more often by design. I know of blind people who run rivers, though they always have someone along who can see. You can feel subsurface currents with the oars or paddles better than you can see them with your eyes. Even taste may be involved in running rapids. I can still taste the dry-mouth, dull-metal flavor of fear from some of the ones I have run.

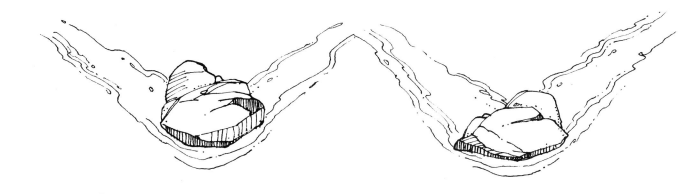

Managing the Craft

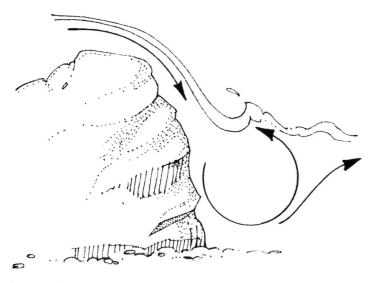

Souse hole

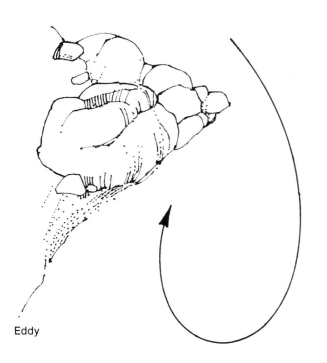

Eddy

There may be times on the river when you want to hit a rock, or go into a hole, or catch an eddy. Generally, however, the name of the game is to avoid obstacles. Avoiding obstacles requires a combination of two skills: reading the water and maneuvering the craft. It involves physical strength, an acute sense of timing, and the practical knowledge of when to do what.

Ferrying is the term used to describe moving across the current. Since the current provides most of the power for river running, selecting the right current is critical to avoiding obstacles. A front ferry involves turning the craft slightly toward the direction you want to move, then using the proper strokes to move the craft forward (downstream). A back ferry involves doing essentially the opposite — turning the craft away from the direction you want to go and using the proper strokes to move backward (upstream). The current helps move the craft the way you want to go.

Turns are accomplished in a variety of ways, depending largely upon the type of craft and the means of control. You can do a back paddle or oar stroke on one side, a front stroke on the other side. In an eddy turn you use the slower water (or reverse current) to move one end or side of the craft while the main current works on the opposite end or side. You assist the various currents with the proper oar or paddle stroke, slowing or speeding up that portion of the craft that needs it to complete the turn.

Eddies

Eddies are reverse currents, water that flows counter to the general flow of the river. They are created by the river seeking its dynamic equilibrium. They occur below barriers that change the level and direction of flow. An eddy can be a dangerous spot to avoid or can be an aid in negotiating the river. Eddies are places to rest and to wait for other party members as a safeguard for their passage through a rapid. They may be

used to help move you across the current, or even upstream, to gain a better angle to move into a rapid.

Kayakers, more than anyone else, use eddies for resting as they play their way downriver, but experienced canoeists also use them for making eddy turns as they pick their way through rapids. The eddy line, because of the adjacent downstream and upstream currents, is a very useful place from which to maneuver a craft.

Polers make use of eddies to move upstream as the members of the Lewis and Clark expedition did on their cross-continental trek. Eddies below rocks, confluence currents, ledge systems, or shallow gravel bars offer good fishing holes. Water changes direction in eddies, often slowing down, dropping its suspended load to form a sandy bottom, which at lower water becomes a beach. Driftwood collects in eddies too, frequently providing a supply of ready firewood near that sandy beach.

Mild eddies make good launching sites, landing sites, and often offer the best anchorages at campsites. They may be safe swimming holes for the party to play in, but watch out for dangerous undertows.

PADDLING   Kayak

Paddles are used to power and control kayaks, canoes, rafts, and johnboats. Kayaks are paddled with double-bladed paddles and canoes are paddled with single-bladed paddles. Some crafts, such as K-1s (one-person kayaks) and C-1s (one-person decked canoes), small rafts, and small open canoes, are often operated by a single paddler. If these smaller boats have more than one paddler, the techniques vary slightly.

Simply, one uses the paddle to move the water in a direction opposite to that in which the craft, or part of the craft, is intended to move. Get out on the river and practice. Take a river trip with someone who knows proper technique. Take a class, join a club, and try to get some good instruction before you attempt something too difficult.

Eric Evans, who dominated slalom kayaking during the 1970s, says there are only four basic strokes for beginning kayakers: the forward paddle stroke, the backward stroke, the sweep stroke, and the draw. Walt Blackadar, the Idaho physician who made big-water kayaking so popular, said that in essence there are only three: forward, back, and draw.

The forward paddle stroke is made by pulling with the bottom hand while pushing with the top hand. In effect, a paddler inserts the paddle into the water and pulls himself forward to the paddle. The blade should be totally underwater for greatest efficiency, and the upper arm will be straightened at the end of the stroke as the lower arm was straight at the beginning of the stroke. Put your whole body into the stroke. Back and trunk muscles are used more than the arm muscles. The stroke is then repeated on the opposite side with the other end (blade) of the paddle in a similar fashion.

The backward stroke is simply the reverse of the forward stroke. The back of the paddle blade (convex surface for a curved paddle) pushes the water rather than the front (concave) surface. You push forward with the bottom hand and pull back (into the body) with the upper

77

hand. As you look over your shoulder to see better, use the same side rather than alternating sides, or you may become disoriented.

The sweep stroke is a basic turning stroke which starts as a forward or backward stroke, but rather than pulling or pushing the paddle in the plane of the kayak, this stroke forms a big arc away from the bow or stern.

The draw stroke moves the kayak sideways. Placing the blade in the water out from the side of the craft, with the top hand almost directly above the bottom hand, you pull the kayak toward the shaft. If you think of yourself as wearing a kayak, rather than merely sitting in it, you may be able to better understand kayak strokes.

Bracing strokes are used to keep balance in the kayak or decked canoe by applying pressure to the river surface or parallel to that surface. The paddler is literally leaning on the paddle as it pushes the water down to keep the paddler up. Hip flexibility plays a key role in kayak paddling and in paddling decked canoes. Most of the movements in paddling involve the whole body.

The Eskimo roll is a technique normally associated with kayaking. It is difficult to learn on your own and is best learned through instruction in a warm swimming pool. Invented by the Eskimo, whose life depended upon his ability to roll upright out of frigid Arctic waters, the roll reduces the kayaker's time wasted swimming. The kayak is a tipsy craft and is designed to roll over and back up, an action that depends entirely upon the paddler.

Canoe

Canoeing strokes are similar to kayak strokes but employ a single-bladed paddle. The same principles hold true. For forward strokes, you place the paddle into the water ahead of you and pull the canoe toward it. For backward strokes, you place the paddle in the water beside you and push backwards away from it.

Similarly, you pry the boat away from the paddle with a pry stroke, pushing the craft away from an imaginary pole

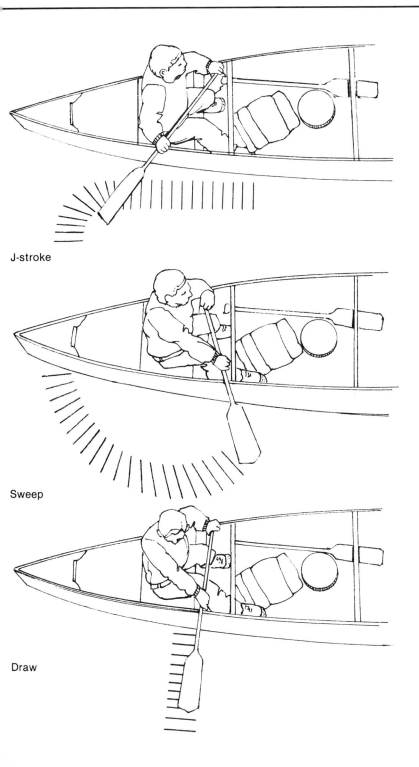

J-stroke

Sweep

Draw

planted near the canoe, and you draw the craft toward the paddle planted at a distance from the canoe in a draw stroke. Other strokes are variations of these and can best be mastered in a class. These variations include sweeps, bow draws, the J-stroke used by the stern paddler as a rudder, and skulling strokes that trace the figure eight. I cannot say enough about joining a paddle club or getting expert instruction. Reading is valuable, but only proper training and experience can make you into a competent paddler.

Keep in mind that there are open canoes and decked canoes, the latter designed for serious whitewater paddling conditions similar to those of kayaking. Such decked canoes have been run successfully through the Grand Canyon, and while I have seen open canoes with spray covers on the Main Salmon, such craft are not meant for Class IV and Class V water unless they are paddled by experts. Even experts have to be a little out of their minds to be in really big water with an open canoe. I do not recommend it.

Inflatable canoes and kayaks (generally less maneuverable and less responsive than their hard-hulled cousins) are paddled much the same way as regular canoes and kayaks, but none of the inflatables that I know of are appropriate for the Eskimo roll. Most are paddled with the double-bladed paddle from a sitting position.

Raft

Paddle rafting has sprung into popularity during the past decade. Several people sit on the tubes of an inflated raft, each with a paddle in hand, and cling to the slippery raft with their feet and legs. A well-trained crew is beautiful to watch, and participants on paddle-powered trips seem to have a lot more fun than passengers on oar-powered rafts who simply sit while the person at the oars does all the work.

Only two basic paddle strokes are really needed—the forward and back strokes. On a command given by whoever is selected captain, the whole crew paddles forward or backward. "Right turn" immediately galvanizes the paddlers on the right into a back paddle stroke while those on the left side paddle forward. Since the left side of the craft will move faster than the right side, the craft will turn to the right. "Left turn" reverses the roles. Often the captain or a guide will sit in the stern of the craft to exert power in whichever direction seems most appropriate to fine-tune the turn.

While paddle rafting provides greater opportunity for participation, paddle rafts are generally less maneuverable than oar- or sweep-powered rafts. If paddle-powered rafts are used for hauling, there is much greater possibility of injury to paddlers from contact with hard-surfaced gear. Many short (one or two day) trips include paddle rafts. If most of the gear is carried on accompanying oar-powered support rafts, extended trips are possible.

Paddle rafting is popular in warmer climates and less common on cold-water rivers and in cooler climates because paddle-raft passengers tend to get wetter than oar- or sweep-powered rafters.

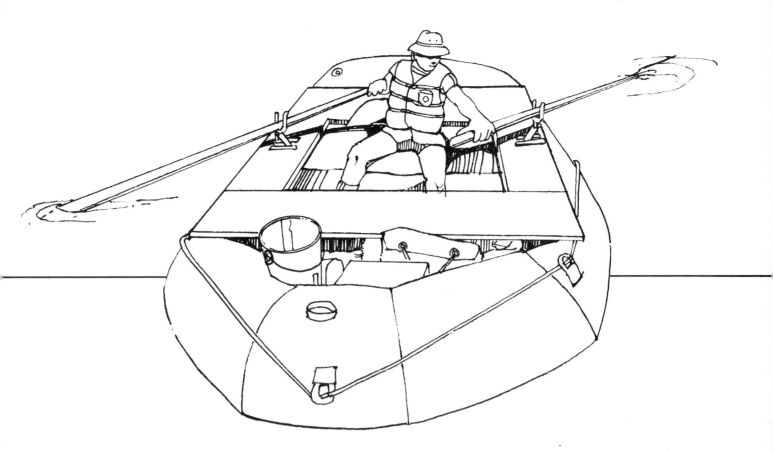

Rowing

Rowing is much the same for any craft you use—dory, sportyak, or raft. Both the dory and the sportyak have built-in oar locks. A few small rafts do too, but they are often inadequate. Larger rafts and pontoons must be equipped with rowing frames on which oar locks of some kind are mounted. Occasionally, with very large craft or in whitewater, two sets of oars may be used. In some big-water river running, a trio of smaller craft are lashed together to form what is known as a triple-rig, with an oar mounted on each of the end boats. The craft is controlled much like a sweep craft.

Again, the principles of paddling hold true. If the rower is facing downstream and pulling back on the oars in hand, the blades in the water move downstream, pushing the water downstream and thereby moving the boat upstream (a maneuver that the rower might use to slow down). Turns can be made by pivoting the craft, which is done by pulling on one oar and pushing on the other.

The basic technique calls for rowing the craft back and forth across the current to select the proper path for the craft. Whatever turns may be necessary are made by pulling and/or pushing on the proper oar. Unless the craft is too heavily loaded with gear and people, it can normally be turned quickly, usually with a single paired movement of the oars. The small sportyak is infinitely maneuverable with its short oars. Dories are quicker to respond than rafts, but good rafts respond easily if they are loaded properly.

Pulling the inboard ends of the oars creates greater power than pushing them. Consequently, the most powerful stroke can be made when the rower wants to go in a direction opposite to the way he is facing. This is ideal for running rivers, as the rower can face downstream or toward the obstacle to be avoided.

The craft can be moved in any direction by changing the angle of the craft in relation to the current and letting the current do most of the work. You can do an upstream or downstream ferry using the power stroke, or you can portegee (after Portuguese fisherman's technique), a rowing technique used to move a boat forward by pushing on the oars.

Sweeping

Poling

Sweeps, long fulcrums with a large blade at the water end, have been used on American rivers for centuries to maneuver boats. In the early days, they were used extensively on scows for downriver freight traffic on the great inland waterways drained by the mighty Mississippi. The sweeps are mounted fore and aft and are handled by one sweepman located near the center of the craft or by two sweepmen, one near each end. I began my river running career as a sweepman on a two-man sweep boat.

Similar to oars in principle, sweeps serve as moveable double rudders, one at each end. The inboard end of the sweep — sometimes counter-weighted so as not to be too heavy to handle — is moved in one direction, which moves the sweep in the water in the opposite direction. The boat (or that end of it) moves in the direction the inboard end of the sweep is moved. Lined up parallel with the current, the craft is moved laterally across the river.

While sweep-controlled craft may seem primitive, they are used on the Middle Fork of the Salmon to negotiate some of the most difficult rapids in the West at low water levels. When operated by a single sweepman, sweeps are likely to be used on freight barges rather than on passenger-carrying craft. Many commercial outfitters in the West use sweeps, for they can negotiate narrow slots on small, tight rivers.

Voyageurs and bargemen developed the technique of poling in the United States and Canada. Devotees to the sport contend that it is not only the best way to negotiate small, shallow streams, but is also the fastest way to travel both upstream and downstream in a canoe.

The technique involves applying power to the solid bottom of the river rather than to the moving water, although poles can also be used just like paddles except for strokes requiring feathering. With the development of the aluminum pole in the mid-1960s, the dying sport seems to have been revived, largely due to the activities of the Beletz brothers — Al, Syl, and Frank — in Missouri.

Polers stand near the middle of the canoe or johnboat, using a pole 10 to 14 feet long. Various end attachments may be used for different bottom conditions. The pole is dropped into the water ahead of the craft. The poler pushes on the pole against the bottom, then moves his hands in a climbing action, hand over hand, until the end of the pole is reached.

If the water becomes too deep for the pole, you simply use the pole as a paddle. The long pole in the water finds enough resistance to produce a powerful thrust, even if it does not contact the bottom.

"Snubbing" is used for moving downstream and involves jabbing the pole into the bottom to slow the craft and to control its movements. Major rapids can be negotiated in this manner. Wes Felty, a self-taught poler in Washington State, makes frequent runs by canoe of Boulder Drop on the Skykomish River (a Class V rapid that is considered one of the toughest in the state).

Traveling upstream, the poler makes use of eddies and the quiet water near shore, but rapids are no problem unless the drops are too steep to negotiate. The current is used to a much greater extent than in any other kind of river boating.

Turns are accomplished by pushing at an angle against the bottom to move the bow in one direction, the stern in the other with the poler at the center of the craft acting as a fulcrum. Experienced polers make use of the lean of the boat to carve their turns, almost like a skier. Most pole-pushers work on only one side of the craft (the traditonal method), but the aluminum and plastic poles have made many new strokes and techniques possible.

AT THE RIVER

The tiny town of Ohiopyle seemed to serve only one purpose — to launch river trips. A whitewater equipment shop full of kayaks, canoes, and accessories dominated the scene as we drove into town over a bridge across the Youghiogheny. Here a dozen small inflatable rafts lay in the shade where a small group of river runners briefed a much larger party of dudes on what was going to happen on the river. A previously-briefed party carried its rafts across the road to the river as a third party began to form around a truck and unload more rafts at another shady spot.

Since we were early, we walked to the river to watch the launch, which had to wait until an earlier party got out of the way. It was a bit of a mob scene, but orderly and organized. Yet it was nothing like the mob scene we experienced on the river where groups of twelve boats, each full of paying passengers, leap-frogged down the river, boats careening off rocks, flipping over in Charlie's Washing Machine, and hanging up on sleepers. People were in the water, some stopping to swim a rapid in their PFDs. It was like Coney Island, great fun and as safe as common sense, lack of booze, and the accompanying kayak safety patrol could dictate.

The next day we tried the Cheat river, and we were all alone with two small boats for six people: Fish and his friend, my wife and I, and her brother and his wife. We had spent the night in a nearby motel and drove to the river at Albright to meet Fish, who had brought the boats in a van. We used the van for the shuttle: Fish, Jess, and Elizabeth drove to Jenkinsburg in two vehicles while Willa, Dolores, and I inflated the boats and rigged them for the river. Leaving the van at the take-out point, they drove back in the other car.

We launched at noon, had a leisurely trip on a hot summer day, stopped to eat, to swim, to swing on the rope at the bridge, and to recover after Willa took an unexpected swim in Coliseum Rapid. It was getting dark before we had de-rigged, deflated the boats, and put them and the gear into the van.

The trip to and from the river can add a whole new dimension to the river trip as you drive along the river or fly over it. When we ran the Cheat, we had time during the shuttle to wander around the little town of Albright, where we discovered America in a local cemetery, in a service station-grocery (we bought a big orange and an RC Cola), and in coal trucks headed for the power plant.

Travel

For the trip to the river, be sure that you start out with, or can purchase along the way, everything you will need. Use check lists. You may develop your own from a sample which can be revised by your personal experience. Make several copies and keep one handy for additions during the trip.

Part of your research has been discovering what is available at or near the put-in in the way of ice, beer, fresh produce, meats, fishing licenses, and other last minute purchases. Don't forget the frozen items you have stashed away in the freezer and any garden vegetables

you planned to bring along.

Load the craft for safe traveling and anticipate rain by having enough tarps along to protect the load. Hard-hulled craft are tied to the vehicle fore and aft, as well as over the belly, and are padded to prevent their rubbing against each other or against any hard surfaces. In-flatables are loaded so that they will not be chafed by ropes or hard surfaces. All tarps and rope ends should be tied so that they will not flap and fray.

Vans and pickup trucks are excellent for carrying equipment and for pulling trailers. Larger four-wheel vehicles may

Shuttle

be necessary for some put-ins and take-outs. I can actually haul more gear on my Toyota Corolla than I can in a Dodge Aspen V8. If gas mileage is a factor (it is for me) and power unimportant, use as small a vehicle as you can.

For loading canoes, kayaks, and sportyaks, use a car-top carrier. I use metal clamps that fit the rain gutters rigged with a pair of 2x4s for carrying canoes, and I use the frame and floor of my rafts as a rack for the rolled raft, ammo boxes, and ice chests. Standard luggage racks are rarely adequate for carrying much weight. Various plastic foam carriers that have come into use during the past few years seem to work well and are easy to remove between trips. You can pack bulky light-weight gear and paddles into the canoe or kayak for the trip to the river.

If you are using a wooden boat, you may want a trailer designed to haul the craft. Many rafters have small trailers to haul their rolled inflatable boats and gear to the river. All gear carried in open trucks and trailers should be tarped and/or tied in. Oars, paddles, poles, and sweeps can be tied to roof-top racks or to trucks and trailers, preferably with the blades to the rear. Be sure such items tied to trailers allow room for turns without damage. Check the load after a few miles to be sure everything is riding properly. Then roll for the river.

Unless you can figure out some way to take your car with you, you will have to arrange a shuttle to get your vehicle from the put-in to the take-out. You may do the shuttle before the trip, but you will always have one vehicle at the put-in, unless you hire a driver. You can spot one vehicle — or even a bike or motorcycle — at the take-out to enable you to do the shuttle after the trip. When my time is limited, I usually hire a shuttle driver to do the work.

Shuttle drivers can be expensive. On the Main Salmon in Idaho, my shuttle for a 10-day, 200-mile trip cost $125 plus gas; but it saved 24 hours of driving time and the hassles of three shuttle trips. Commercial outfitters and livery services will often have off-duty guides and employees willing to do the job for reasonable rates.

Leaving a car at either the put-in or the take-out has its risks, unless you can arrange for someone to watch the vehicles, keep them parked under surveillance, and deliver them to the take-out at the time of anticipated arrival. On Alaskan and Canadian trips involving float planes, the logistics are dependent upon others, but you need to check carefully concerning your pick-up arrangements and take along extra food for the possibility of your pick-up plane being weathered in. Your very life could depend upon it.

Rigging

Rigging is simple for the one- and two-person craft — the canoe, kayak, small raft, and sportyak. You take them off the vehicle, tie on grab loops and painters (bow and stern lines), and add flotation units. Much of the rigging gear may stay with the craft so it is virtually river ready at all times. Some river runners even keep sponges and bailing buckets, PFDs, and paddles attached to the craft in storage.

Inflatables need to be pumped up. If an electric outlet or generator is available, you can use an electric blower, an old vacuum cleaner, or a hair-drier to inflate the craft. If not, use a muscle powered pump. You will want to take a foot- or hand-pump to top off (add pressure to) the boat during the trip. Cool water reduces expansion pressure. Be sure inflatables are tight even in cold water and cold weather. Air pressure may have to be bled off later in the day when the temperature rises.

Johnboat and dory trailers can be backed right into the river at many launch sites, but without this access, the craft will have to be manhandled into the water. Some dories and johnboats may be nested for efficient hauling to the river and must be rigged with compartments and seats.

Inflatable craft using oars and sweeps need to be married to their means of power and control. Frames are strapped, roped, or chained to the D-rings on the craft. Floors and poop decks are then fastened to frames and/or other D-rings. Oar-locks or sweep-mounts are part of the frame of rafts, but they are part of the craft in sportyaks, dories,

and johnboats. Ropes that serve as grab lines, bow and stern lines, and grab loops need to be tied in place and checked, and auxiliary equipment, such as bailing buckets and throw lines, should be tied in before the craft is loaded with gear.

Most rigging is done before the craft is in the water. However, stepping on or walking around in hard-hulled craft on land can be structurally damaging and may reduce the life of the boat. I stand on foam pads placed on the floor when pumping my raft. Most rafts can be inflated without getting inside the craft. Your pump air hose should be long enough. Do not use the raft itself as a base for the pump, as the friction of the operating pump will wear the fabric.

Packing

Most of the packing will have been done at home, but there will always be last minute additions: purchases made on the way to the river, items thrown into the vehicle at the last minute, and assorted gear that doesn't seem to fit anywhere. If the party meeting at the river is coming from different directions, there will be the need to sort out gear and food. On the Salmon River trip, we had people converging on the river from

Washington State and Washington, D.C., from San Francisco, Santa Barbara, and Grand Canyon.

Unloading the vehicles at the river can be organized so that the gear is logically planned and physically placed to facilitate loading the craft. The packing at the river consolidates gear and equipment, a process which continues during the trip as the party shakes down and people come to know where key items are located. Checklists come in handy. It helps to camp near the launch site the night before to facilitate the repacking.

It is important that the "captain" of every craft and the leader of the party know where everything is packed and just what is on each boat. Checklists help here, too. If each craft carries the same items each day, their loading is more efficient. Breakable items and hard, sharp external surfaces need to be padded to prevent their causing damage or being damaged. Just as you will pack heavy containers low when you load the craft, so you pack all heavy items low within their containers.

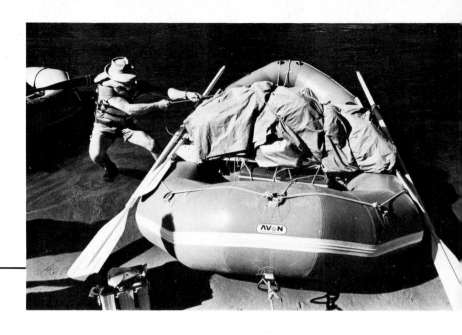

Loading

Heavy items should be packed low, and the craft trimmed (balanced) fore and aft, as well as laterally with allowances made for passenger weight. Rafts and dories may be overloaded at one end to balance the passenger load at the other. Dories with compartments need to be carefully loaded in balance. Canoes are prone to capsize unless properly loaded. Poop decks on rafts raise the raft's center of gravity. Floors suspended from D-rings or rowing frames that make use of interior space in the raft lower the center of gravity. Suspended netting can also be used for hauling gear low in the boat.

Everything should be tied in for most trips. Some canoeists advise against this, pointing out that it tends to make pinned craft harder to rescue. Unless you are willing to lose gear, it had better be tied in.

Before you put anything into the boats, clean it off. Before you put yourself into the boat, clean yourself off. The mud and sand you track into the boat will not only get your gear dirty, it will also act like an abrasive and wear out the boat's fabric. It is better to load craft in the water than on shore. Don't overload them. Even the stable raft is more likely to flip with an improperly balanced load than a well-packed one. Overloaded craft are also hard to maneuver.

Inflatables need to be pumped tight to maneuver properly. If the tubes are soft or the frame sags with the load, top off the tubes. The extra flotation in kayaks and canoes needs to be in place and secured before you are river-ready.

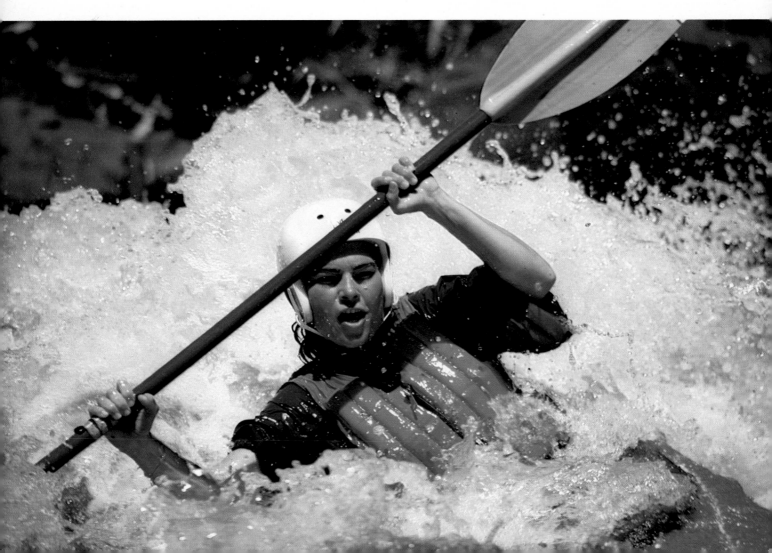

Launching

Many popular rivers have well-established launching sites. As some are better than others, a few guidelines are worth mentioning for selecting a launch site. If possible, launch in still water rather than in swift current. Launch from solid ground rather than from swampy, muddy, slippery ground or from logs or rocks. Launch in water deep enough to float the craft so that you won't have to get wet. If you do have to wade into the river, dress for it by wearing the proper footgear. Not that you shouldn't ever get wet. Most river campers will, eventually, but there is no need to be unnecessarily uncomfortable. Besides, deep-water launches are easier on the craft.

Be sure that you are ready to launch when you shove off, that all gear is aboard and properly stowed, that everyone is accounted for, that everyone is wearing a PFD, and that everyone has been briefed on safety practices and river routine. Once in the water, it will pay (in reduced wear and tear on the craft) to lift rather than drag the craft across rocky beaches, through beaver-cut willows, and over flooded rock gardens.

On the Green River in Dinosaur National Monument a few years ago, on a trip with David Sumner, we were ready to launch by 7 a.m. for a race to the take-out. Our boat was beached. Instead of lifting it (it was quite heavy), we pushed and shoved. The pressure of the tightly-pumped inflatable boat against an underwater rock shattered the sandstone and a sliver of rock pierced one air chamber with a whoosh that left the craft crippled. By the time we had unloaded, patched, and launched it again, it was 11 a.m. We had lost four hours — and the race.

Etiquette

With the explosion in river use that has occurred during the past few decades, river etiquette becomes ever more important. There will be more people using the rivers. That's a fact of life. Most etiquette is just common sense and human dignity that has become common practice. It means leaving campsites as clean as we find them, perhaps improved for our having been there. It means throwing nothing into the river, not even cigarette butts or fish offal.

But it also means treating other people with respect and dignity. You don't move in on another party's campsite. By the same token, you don't take up three campsites with one party at popular camping areas. You respect the quiet and solitude of the river experience by leaving radios and tape decks at home.

Be aware of people's sensitivities and respect them. Taking off your clothes among friends is one thing, among strangers is another. Nudity occurs on many rivers, but better kept within the party and not flaunted. It can even get you into trouble, as it did with the party on the Green River in Dinosaur National Monument that was cited for not wearing PFDs. That was taking nudity too far for the National Park Service.

Wrap-Up

The take-out can be more crowded than the put-in. If you have ever seen a river trip disembark, you know what it can be like — a dozen clowns coming out of a VW at the circus. You can't believe all the gear and equipment, boxes, bags, and bundles — and it all has to be organized and packed back into the waiting vehicles. Things are chaotic at best while everything is unloaded and dumped onto the shore. Boats are de-rigged, scrubbed down, sponged off, and hauled out of the river to dry and be loaded for the trip home.

Meanwhile, all the gear is sorted and separated, packed and loaded, while the trash, garbage, ash, and human waste are properly disposed of (all but the human waste in the trash cans — human waste in special facilities). A careful policing of the area is important, not only to keep it clean, but to keep track of all equipment and personal items. It is wise to keep all of your party's gear together so that it won't be lost or stolen.

So the river trip is over. You say goodbye to the river, to your old friends and new ones. There is a letdown, a sense of loss, of anticlimax. If you have been gone several days, there is cultural shock upon returning to civilization. As much as you may want a hot shower, a cheeseburger, and a chocolate malt, you feel cheated somehow when it is all over but the drive home.

HEALTH & SAFETY

Before Mount St. Helens blew her top, there was a river called the Toutle in Washington state that offered a fantastic whitewater run of some fifteen miles. The river is still there, but the May 18, 1980 eruption has changed its nature so drastically that the run is only a memory. Where there were once Class IV rapids in a lovely basaltic gorge, there are now sand waves in the midst of high mud banks and scattered logjams.

We ran the Toutle one rainy spring weekend in April 1980. Saturday was somewhat sunny, and we could see the mountain smoking in the distance. On Sunday, when we had paying passengers, showers fell off and on all day. Saturday's run was exciting but uneventful. Sunday's run was quite the opposite.

Everything was fine until we reached the Steps, a tightly packed series of Class IV rapids. I was leading in the rowing rig followed by four smaller rafts paddled by the paying passengers with a guide at the rudder position in the stern of each. Pete, in the last boat, was one paddler short of a full complement.

As the last boat negotiated the first drop, it missed the slot and plowed sideways over a rock into a pour-over with a small stopper. This hydraulic stopped the boat, catapulting five passengers into the raging river. Pete, well braced in the stern and anticipating the jolt, had stayed with the boat. He was still upright but was having a tough time controlling the boat by himself. Five people were in the river in various states of panic. The parents of one of the five were in my raft.

The water was terribly cold. As lead boat carrying food and gear for the day trip, I was also the safety boat carrying the throw line. I was having a hard time trying to run the technical rapids while staying in position to help in the rescue. I did not want anyone in the water passing me.

I watched three people wash toward a house-sized boulder with a dead cedar tree lodged against it on the upstream side. Happily, they all washed free. Then I saw a woman reach the righthand shore where Kyle's boat picked her up. Another passenger swept toward me at amazing speed, and I was able to get the throw line to him, pull him in, and catch an eddy where I waited. I broke out the dry clothes for the shivering victim while I watched for others.

None came. I landed, tied up, and made sure that the wet passenger was all right. Then I started hiking upstream. I saw Kyle's boat in an eddy across the river. Kyle knew no more than I did. I motioned them downstream to rendezvous with my boat to get dry clothes for the woman, who was shaking uncomfortably.

I continued upstream, worried. I must have hiked a quarter-mile before I saw another boat. Everything was under control. All passengers were out of the river, but they were wet and cold. All the boats had stopped, and dry passengers had shared clothing with wet ones. We negotiated the rest of the Steps, stopped on an island, and built a huge, warming, drying fire. Then we broke out lunch. The fire, food, and dry clothes saved the day.

Water Hazards

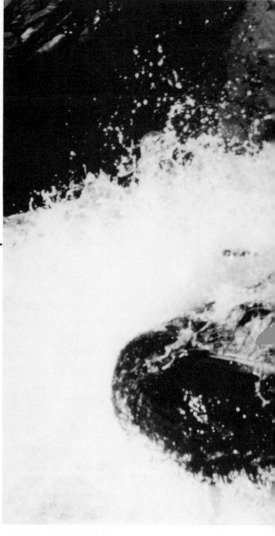

There is always a possibility on whitewater river trips that a craft will be swamped, capsized, pinned or wrapped, dumped, or will entrap someone. A pin or a wrap involves a craft being held against some obstacle by the force of the current. Entrapment is the holding of someone by a tree, snag, rock, or reversal current. River runners must learn to recognize potential hazards and avoid them. That is why reading water is so important.

Sweepers are trees or other obstacles in or above the water that might sweep a person out of a boat. Sleepers are nearly hidden, slightly submerged rocks or logs difficult to see because they cause little surface turbulence but can capsize a craft or hang it up.

Hydraulics are the wildly dramatic movements of the water as it responds to obstacles. They have wonderful names such as haystacks, waves, souse holes, stoppers, roosters (for rooster tails), and holes. The latter are depressions in the surface of the water caused by boulders or other obstacles to the downstream flow.

Rapids occur where the river's downstream flow is blocked or slowed by rock debris, ledge systems, or other objects, natural or man-made. Low dams are another form of rapids. They are often deadly due to their fierce reversal currents that can hold boats and bodies and recirculate them for days.

Flash floods and reservoir releases can also affect you on the river or in camp. High water flows faster than low water and is usually colder, whether due to reservoir release or snowmelt runoff. Low water flows slower but exposes more obstacles.

Overboard

An amazing number of people on river trips go overboard without any serious consequences. It should cause concern at first, however, because a person in the water is generally out of control, an unpleasant and disconcerting situation.

If you find yourself in the water, let your PFD do its job. Do not try to swim. Don't panic. Keep your mind about you. Do not try to stand in moving water. If you get a foot caught between rocks, you can drown in two feet of water.

Roll onto your back with a sculling stroke (circular movement of the hands), point your feet downstream to ward off rocks, and keep them near the surface to avoid entrapment. Type I PFDs will float you face-up. You will only have to control the direction of your body in relation to the current, which will carry you along, usually faster than the craft you just left.

When overboard, you will want to stay with the boat, but be careful to avoid getting trapped between the craft and a downstream rock. People in the craft should help you back into the boat.

In extremely cold water, you may want to head for shore to avoid or to treat hypothermia. Your party should also head for shore. It is best to have some waterproof matches along, perhaps in a pocket sewn into your PFD.

Pinned

Pinning is temporary and wrapping is more permanent. Both mean that a craft is held against some obstacle by the current. Immediate action is vital to prevent a capsize in most pinning situations. Try to keep the craft moving and shift weight to the downriver side of the craft (which is the side that lies against or upon the obstacle).

The most immediate natural reaction is to lean away from the obstacle, but that places added weight on the upstream side, which is already lower due to the impact. If the gunwale of a rigid craft, such as a canoe or dory, goes under water, it will flip or be wrapped around the obstacle with the full force of the current playing against it. Rafts, because of their stable nature, are more likely to spin off, although they, too, can flip and wrap.

If a craft wraps, people may end up still in the craft, dumped in the water, or stranded on the obstacle. Those in the river should be rescued first. People trapped underwater are an immediate priority. Throw lines from other boats or from parties on shore can be used, but never tie anyone to a rope. The current could force the person under water.

Several methods of self-rescue may be tried. At first bounce the craft and shift weight. Use the oars to catch the current in combination with a weight shift. Stand on the obstacle and lift the craft (be careful not to be pinned if it moves). Search and rescue teams may have to be called. If all else fails, the stranded people may have to swim. This is not a very pleasant notion but better than starving to death on a mid-stream rock.

If forced to swim out, use the position of the stranded craft and the current to reach shore. Organize the party before you leave the craft and take along whatever you need for the walk out.

To recover the craft, make use of ropes and the force of the current. Tie ropes securely around seats, thwarts, or D-rings. Use a combination of anchor points to distribute stress. A block-and-tackle is often useful in this operation and it pays to have plenty of strong, extra rope.

Occasionally, a craft will have to be abandoned, at least until the water level drops or rises, which may be a matter of hours or months. Human life is more important than any craft.

Capsized

Kayakers anticipate capsize and learn to roll back to an upright position. Sport-yakers expect to upset occasionally — it goes with the territory. Canoeists of anything but the mildest flat-water river know that sooner or later they will swamp (fill the craft with water) and perhaps capsize. All of these craft should have some natural or built-in flotation, and all of them can, and

should, have additional flotation installed if they are to be used in heavy whitewater.

Dories, while infinitely maneuverable, are not as stable as the relatively sluggish raft and will flip easier. Rafts and dories will still float when they are full of water, but they become hard to handle. Johnboats are stable but are rarely used in heavy whitewater.

Swamped boats may remain upright, but often become unmanageable and hazardous to anyone in the water. Avoid becoming trapped between a

swamped craft and a rock or other obstacle. Operators should stay with their boats (staying upstream of them) and should work them to shore or into an eddy as soon as possible. Other members of the party can help, unless they are in trouble themselves, which is a good reason to run most hazardous waters in a well-planned pattern.

A capsized craft and its former occupants are under the river's power. It litters the water with everything that has not been tied down, which confuses the people in the water. They don't know whether to save gear or themselves. Save yourself first. A number of drownings have occurred when people tried to grab insignificant items and lost themselves.

Most craft can be righted in the water, but it is usually easier on shore or in shallow water near shore. Members of the party who have not been capsized should do as much as possible, because the victims may be hypothermic or in shock and may not recognize their own exhaustion. They should be treated with all consideration and watched carefully. Deal with hypothermia before you try to right the craft. If secured, it won't go away.

Crafts should be bailed as much as possible if they are upright. Inverted boats will have little water in them when they are set upright but should be bailed dry. At most, they might need to be unloaded and repacked. At least, they should be checked thoroughly for damage and shifting cargo. Rafts may need to be rigged all over again and unpacked. Capsizes can be time-consuming, causing lengthy delays.

Entrapped

Entrapment is the most terrifying possibility for whitewater river runners. In a strange way, it is even more frightening than drowning. Most river runners who have been at it for long know of at least one entrapment case. The professional river people can deal with drowning because they are sure they can avoid it, but entrapment can happen in spite of everything you may do correctly.

Entrapment can be caused by solid surface objects like sweepers, rocks, and logjams, but people and craft can also be trapped in hydraulics caused by underwater obstacles. Stoppers, keepers, souse holes, and reversals are all names for deep holes in which currents are moving violently upstream. People and boats can become trapped in them and recirculate for minutes, even hours.

Don't get into keepers if you can avoid them. If you get into them, your best bet may be to get out of the boat, if you are still in it, and even get out of your PFD, so you can swim down into the deeper currents that flow through. This is sometimes the only way to get out. Self rescue may be the only rescue, but parties should be prepared with safety lines and throw ropes. Kayakers can serve as safety patrols to help out in hydraulic entrapment, and many commercial rafting outfitters use them in that capacity.

No craft or person on the river is immune to entrapment. Kayakers have died when their craft became wedged beneath an underwater log and they could not extract themselves. Walt Blackadar, one the most famous big-water kayakers in North America, died when his kayak was caught under a log on the South Fork of the Payette River in Idaho a few years ago. I have seen a canoeist drown when his craft wrapped against a bridge piling, trapping him underwater where no one could reach him. A commercial guide drowned in Grand Canyon when his life jacket became entangled with the motor mount of a huge pontoon as the craft flipped in Upset Rapid.

Because there is so little that can be done for the entrapment victim, the old "ounce of prevention" adage is especially important. Avoid entrapment by carefully reading the river, by scouting rapids, and by planning your course in hazardous waters. Never boat alone.

Some parties practice the proper position for floating, running rapids for fun in their PFDs. The American National Red Cross film "The Uncalculated Risk" graphically illustrates the dangers of trying to stand or walk in moving water.

Prepare yourself for an entrapment before it occurs by knowing how to use throw ropes. Send someone for help if practical assistance is available. Try to reach the victim if it is possible without endangering another life.

The Elements

The rain, sun, and wind all affect river trips. Rain can bring on hypothermia, obliterate the shoreline, cause flash floods, and precipitate colds. Sun can burn, desiccate, blind, and crack lips. Boats can be capsized, blown off course or held up for hours by the wind. The elements demand understanding and must be dealt with.

Rain can be more than just unpleasant. A 14-day trip on the Main Salmon in 1977 was spoiled by 11 consecutive days of rain. Hypothermia in its mildest forms became something we lived with from day to day. It can rain on any river trip in North America. Frequently the storms in areas of little rainfall are more severe than those in rainy climates. Get off the river if it rains too hard.

Select campsites that are well drained and above the high water mark. If lightning accompanies storms, avoid trees, tall rocks, and high places. River corridors offer good theoretical protection from lightning strikes, but thunder roars mightily through the canyons. I prefer snow to rain, unless it is as wet as rain. Dry snow is wonderful on the river, but dress warmly with wool and heavy wet boots for the cold weather.

The sun burns hot on many popular rivers, especially during the summer. Wear sunglasses, wide-brimmed hats, long-sleeved shirts, and long pants. Use sunscreen lotion and suntan oil. Drink plenty of water and seek shade during the heat of the day, even if it means pulling off the river for an hour or two. Know how to recognize sunstroke and heat exhaustion, and avoid them. It is tough to run a technical rapid when reflected sunlight blinds the operator of the craft. Carry along Bag Balm, the river runner's favorite hand cream, or other lotions to treat dry skin and chapped lips. Be prepared to treat sunburn if someone is burned on the river where the reflected light may be as hazardous as direct sun.

The wind always blows upstream on every river I have run, with so few exceptions that I can count them on both hands. You need to learn to read the wind as well as the water to stay on course at times, and there may be occasions when it is best to pull off the river until the wind dies. Gusts in some narrow canyons have been known to lift loaded rafts completely off the water and toss them on shore.

Wind is also a factor at camp. Anticipate the change in direction of wind (from upstream to downstream as the sun goes down) when determining where to locate the campfire in relation to the kitchen and which way to face the tent. Because the wind on many rivers begins blowing upstream as the heat of the day grows, it may be important to get an early start to avoid strong winds. You can also camp early, waiting out the wind in the comfort of camp rather than on the rough river. On the Colorado River in Grand Canyon last spring, we were held up for two hours by forty-mile-an-hour gusts.

Hypothermia

Hypothermia is serious business. People die from it every year. You don't have to get wet to become hypothermic, but wet people on river trips are prime targets. Going overboard is not the only way to lose body heat. Hypothermia can be brought on by too many wave splashes, water fights, or even prolonged rain.

People suffer hypothermia when they lose too much body heat. If getting wet and cold in the winter is a possibility, wear a wet suit. Wet boots are a good idea any time you run cold water rivers. Preparation is the key. Dress appropriately for the river and have the right emergency clothing along. Know how to recognize hypothermia. Be willing to act on what you know — don't take the victim's word for it. Too many people ignore the condition until it has gone too far.

Terminate exposure by getting the afflicted person out of the river and out of wet clothes. Stop the loss of body heat. Get him or her out of the weather and into dry clothes. Put on another layer to hold heat to the body and to prevent any further heat loss.

Food is important in preventing and in treating hypothermia since energy has been lost by the body in the form of heat. People on river trips need to continually replenish their energy reserves, especially if they have to battle cold water, evaporation, wind, and cold weather. High energy food snacks like gorp are good. Meals in general should provide high energy. Total hypothermia treatment includes stopping heat loss, encouraging heat retention, providing extra warmth with additional clothing, a warming fire, and warm drinks. In extreme cases, the victim may have to be warmed through skin-to-skin contact in a sleeping bag.

Remember, hypothermia can kill. It numbs the body and the mind. It makes one shiver, turn blue, and lose control of small muscular movement and then speech. Ultimately mental and physical processes cease. Many rivers in northern latitudes and at high elevations are cold any time of the year because they are fed by snowmelt.

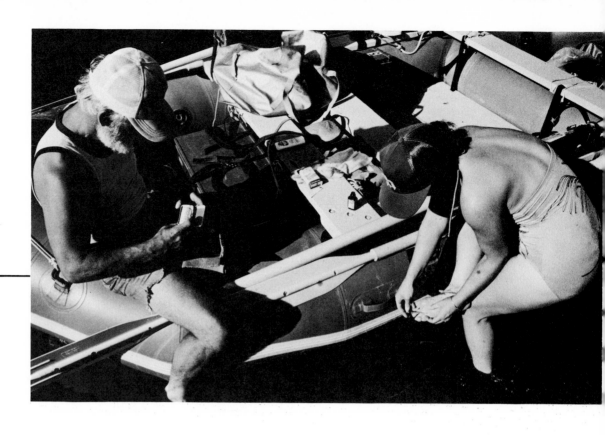

First Aid

Major injuries from violent action can occur on river trips, but most accidents happen off the river, and most are minor. The more serious accidents happen when boats pin or wrap, hit rocks, capsize, or drop into holes. Any sudden stop is likely to throw people around and may hurt them.

Every party should be accompanied by a person trained in first aid who knows what to do when someone is hurt or sick. If anyone on the trip is subject to serious medical problems, a nurse or doctor should be invited along, or the person should not go. Medical problems of everyone on the trip should be known to the trip leader if they might affect other members of the party.

Most medical problems that occur on river trips happen on shore. The most common problems involve insect bites and stings (rarely snake bites), sunburn and other minor burns from cooking or campfires, cuts, scrapes, and bruises. People new to the river routine sometimes develop upset stomachs, diarrhea, or headaches. The failure to drink enough water is a common problem.

If you drink the water of the river you run, or even the water of seemingly pure tributary streams, you may become ill. In recent years, even some of the pure mountain streams of the Rockies have become infected with *Giardia Lamblia*, a flagellated protozoan that causes severe diarrhea.

Most river runners today treat their drinking water with one of several

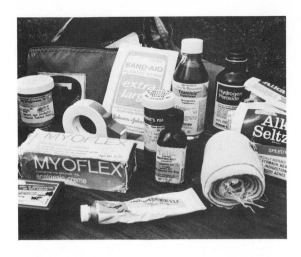

First Aid Kit

methods: Halazone, bleach (Clorox), Globaline, EDWGT (Emergency Drinking Water Germicidal Tablet), or iodine (either tincture or saturated). The water can also be boiled, a very effective treatment, but one that is time- and energy-consuming.

All of the above methods are effective for either clear or cloudy water at 20° C, but according to EPA tests, only Halazone and EDWGT are effective for clear water at 3° C. Boiling is probably the most effective method because *Giardia* cysts are killed immediately by exposure to boiling water.

Such medical problems as heart attack, stroke, and heat exhaustion are relatively rare, but trip leaders and first aid specialists should be on the lookout for potential problems. The first aid kit should reflect the needs of the group, and matters of health should be discussed openly. Poison ivy should be pointed out to those who don't know it.

The first aid kit should be as elaborate as you need to deal with anticipated health problems but within the limits of your first aid ability. There is no need for medication or materials you do not know how to use. On the other hand, you should learn how to use the medication which you might need on the river. Anyone who spends a lot of time isolated from convenient medical attention owes it to companions to know what to do in medical emergencies. If you lead a lot of trips, get some kind of advanced first aid training. Someone along should have American Red Cross First Aid and Cardio-Pulmonary Resuscitation (CPR) training.

A good first aid kit will include the following items:

Splints (I use wire, not pneumatic, splints)
Triangular bandages
Gauze pads (various sizes)
Ace bandages and clips
Sterile gauze and tape
Band-Aids
Scissors/Tweezers
Eyewash and cup plus eye-dressing kit
Antiseptic
Laxative/Antacid
Aspirin
Alka-Seltzer
Bag Balm
Campho-Phenique
Snakebite kit
Tourniquet
Tongue depressors
Iodine, Merthiolate
Alcohol
Hydrogen peroxide
Ammonia inhalants
Sunburn lotions (Foille)
Calamine lotion
Razor blades, safety pins
Antihistamine

RIVER RUNNING

Most people who run whitewater would freely admit to a fear of running rapids. Generally, they don't talk about that fear, except among themselves, most likely around a riverside campfire after a few beers. I recall a 1974 (or was it '73?) river trip when I was guiding for Jim Campbell. We'd stopped to have a look at Wild Sheep Rapid in Hells Canyon, scouting it from an outcrop of living rock. Jim observed, "I never will forget the first time I ran this rapid: it scared hell out of me." Then he paused, thought for a moment as he gazed at the maelstrom below, and added, "It still does."

Ray Ford, scouting Lava Falls in Grand Canyon from river level, returned to the huge black rock where the rest of us were studying the raging rapid from above and said simply, "I don't want to run that," nodding his head toward the 37-foot drop. We watched Rod Nash run it adequately, planned our runs, and followed, each of us getting thrashed a different way, filling rafts to the gunwales but remaining upright to catch the eddy below. We hadn't conquered the rapid, just survived it.

Rapids are the highlights of whitewater river trips, but there are numerous other attractions—early morning light on canyon walls, cloud shadows across the landscape, fresh fish for breakfast, the thrill of camping where Lewis and Clark camped, the rising mist from a north country river on a cold morning that promises a warming sun.

People run rivers for a variety of reasons—to get away from the civilization we have created, to explore isolated places and our inner selves, to experience the quiet solitude of unspoiled places. Paddling a broad Yukon River, you may stop to pan gold, watch a bear fishing the riffle, visit an old village, photograph a moose or a flight of ducks. Johnboating a spring-fed stream in the Ozarks, you stop to fish for your supper, swim in a quiet pool, and then camp beside a reflecting cliff.

Canoeing the interior of Labrador, you may follow the paddle strokes of Olaus Murie, reliving with him the experience of sixty years ago. Rafting a desert river in the Southwest, you may smell the sagebrush cut by bank-dwelling beaver, seek ancient Indian dwellings and rock art as collard lizards skirt the camp and wild horses roam the rim.

Rivers take you somewhere. They tug at the boats tied to the landing, and once you launch—even on a slow river or in a quiet eddy—you soon feel the flow, remarkably fast at times, so fast that until you learn to judge correctly, it may fool you onto a sandbar or into a snag. Running the river and camping along its shores, you will have a few accidents, be inconvenienced, even frightened a bit at times; but you will learn as you store up experiences to tell around the campfire, as you begin to feel the river and sense its liquid spirit, as you respond to its rhythm, and glory in its power.

Routine

So much of what happens on river trips depends upon factors that cannot be controlled, such as weather, water levels, and lateral currents, that everything that can be controlled, should be. The patterns that develop on a trip are important to its success. While it is certainly possible to regiment too much, good organization pays big dividends.

The order of craft is important. The most experienced river runner usually goes last as the sweep boat to follow up on any accident, while the person who knows the river best usually goes first. All other boats remain between them and stay in touch with one another. The leader keeps in sight of the next boat behind, and the sweep boat keeps in sight of the party. This is the ideal pattern and will vary depending upon the experience of the party and conditions on the river. The pattern can be tightened in

Stops

bad weather, with inexperienced people, or in emergency conditions.

Each party should develop a system of signals which should be simple, useable, and understandable. Some means of communication among boats is needed to prevent confusion and to deal with emergencies.

Practice makes perfect, and routines should become practice. If possible, PFDs should be tested. Throw lines should be tried out so that people know how to use them.

Pace is a product of the party, and it may cause conflict among individuals with different senses of time. On some days you may need to push to reach a specific point. That point might be a favorite campsite, a tough rapid at the right water level, or a special lunch stop. If you plan enough time for the trip, you can usually set your own pace, a pace that suits the party as its varying needs become evident — let's fish, let's hike, let's relax.

Nothing can slow a river party more than too many rest stops, and nothing can be as uncomfortable as having too few. Whether or not calls of nature are involved — and they usually are for someone — rest stops every hour or two are important for comfort and solidarity. They enable people to mix rather than be stuck in the same boat too long, and they provide opportunities to stretch cramped legs, to rest tired shoulders, to discuss the next rapid, or to plan the best place for lunch.

Many rest stops will be planned to visit an old homesteader's cabin or abandoned ranch, an Indian battlefield or spectacular waterfall, an old mine or logging camp, a heron rookery or petroglyph site, a historic portage or feral fruit orchard. Portages and rapid-scoutings serve as rest stops, and certain points of progress downriver suggest breaks — the confluence of the Salmon with the Snake in Hells Canyon or the Colorado with the Green in Canyonlands National Park.

Some stops will be unplanned. Out of beer on the St. Croix, we stop at Danville for a supply. A herd of bighorn sheep appears on the right bank and we stop to take pictures. A deer might give us pause. A river rising rapidly due to a distant thunderstorm could either cause a delay or reduce the time it takes to reach a given point. Another party is stopped for lunch, and you see an old friend. You find the perfect beach from which to swim. You need shade during the heat of the day or shelter during a downpour. Perhaps a new rapid has appeared. Warm Springs on the Yampa, Crystal on the Colorado, and Beech Run on the Cheat were all formed overnight.

Lunch

Many parties carry GORP (Good Old Raisins and Peanuts), granola bars, dried fruit, and various snacks to munch on during the day, but paddling, rowing, hiking, exploring, and just being out in the open air will develop appetites for more substantial food.

If lunch is carried in one craft, only this one load need be disturbed. If perishables are involved, they should be easy to get at during the day. If water is needed, it too should be readily available, either at a tributary stream or from a jug. Ease of preparation is the key to the midday meal. It is a time to relax and enjoy, have a swim, explore a tributary, visit a site, and store up needed energy for the afternoon run.

The lunch crew breaks out the meal, opens cans and jars, cuts the salami and summer sausage, the cheese and bread, makes the tuna salad, and mixes the lemonade. Sandwiches of meat, fish, and cheese are common, as are peanut butter and jelly sandwiches, fresh fruit, pickles, olives, chips, crackers, and cookies. Breads may be English muffins, pocket bread, leftover pancakes, or standard sliced loaves. All this is spread out on a cloth on the ground or on a flat rock.

Cleanup involves storing perishables in the ice chest and putting away leftover food. Put any dirty dishes in a bag to wash up that evening rather than dirtying the river by inadequately washing them at lunch. Bag trash and garbage for later disposal. Don't shake out the tarp or table cloth. Instead, use it to funnel the crumbs into the garbage bag to carry out.

118

RAPIDS

Scouting

If you have decent maps, guide books, and knowledge of the river, you will anticipate the rapids. If you can't predict them, you have no business on the river. Some rapids will need to be scouted. If it is your first run, you may want to scout more of them than if you know the river well. A river may be entirely different at different water levels, and rapids can be created overnight. Be prepared to stop and scout if you see anything out of the ordinary. A good rule, a bit tired but still true, is when in doubt, stop and scout.

To scout a rapid, you need to look it over before you run it. Stop above the rapid, normally on shore but possibly on a midstream rock or shelf. Be careful of slick or crumbly rocks when you disembark. It is best to scout from above the water as well as from water level to get a total perspective. The best scouting vantage point may be indicated in your guide or on your map. You can often determine the standard spot by the used trails and landing places.

You can tell when a rapid is close by the sound of its roaring water and by the appearance of the river, which often pools just above a rapid or accelerates at the approaching drop. Stop your craft where it can be safely secured while you scout. Study the current and select a route. Discuss it with your companions and plan how you will negotiate each portion of the rapid.

As you study the rapid, note natural markers such as mid-river rocks, features on shore, curiously-curling waves, or frequently-forming bits of froth that mark hidden rocks.

In oceans, waves more, and the water merely rises and falls as the waves pass through. In rivers, however, the water moves, and the waves stay in the same place because they are formed by underwater obstacles.

Understand the nature of a rapid, and you have a greater appreciation for the best way to run it and a better chance of running it successfully.

When you scout a rapid and find you don't want to run it, there are three options: getting someone else to run your craft through; lining it through; or portaging around the rapid. Lining and portaging will be discussed below. Getting someone else to run your craft is not cowardly. It simply makes sense and is done frequently by commercial outfitters using professional guides.

Neither be afraid to say you don't want to run a particular rapid nor to ask your passengers to walk around. Professional outfitters often have their paying passengers walk around a rapid or give them the choice of walking or running with a craft manned by a team of guides. Never run water you feel is beyond your ability. It is far better to let your companions know you don't feel right about running a rapid than to endanger them and yourself. Your companions may be just as uncertain as you. False bravado can get the whole party into trouble.

Running

Most simply, running the rapid is executing the plan you have developed during the scout, but it requires skill and strength. With the adrenalin flowing there should be plenty of power to call upon. It helps to see another craft run the rapid first. Not all the craft in a party need follow the same route, although in some of the more technical rapids there may be only one basic route, at

least until someone makes a mistake and discovers there are other safe runs (as I did in Boulder Drop on the Skykomish River last spring).

Give yourself plenty of room to maneuver into position. You may have to line a boat upstream or catch an upstream eddy to put your craft into position. Have in mind an alternate route through the maze should you miss your route or catch a rock or a lateral current. Know what to do if you get in trouble anywhere along the way.

Some rapids can be run successfully by merely selecting the proper current to take you through, but in many you will have to move the craft to avoid obstacles. The more technical the rapid, the more maneuvering required. You don't play rock shots (bounce off rocks) by design unless you have an inflatable craft which takes that kind of beating.

A rower will face the bow of the craft toward an obstacle in order to be able to watch it while he rows upstream to ferry the craft safely around the danger. A paddler, on the other hand, will face his craft away and to the side of the obstacle in order to use his paddling to keep the craft clear. Poled and sweep-powered craft depend to a high degree upon the current and the craft's reaction to the current.

Keep the craft moving, but make use of quiet water and eddies if they will help you through. Be ready to react to any deviation from your planned course. Have non-active passengers ready to bail, and use the buddy system for the possibility of anyone going overboard.

Lining and Portaging

In running Crystal Rapid in Grand Canyon, Ray Ford's Avon Pro was spun a quick 180 degrees on the tip of the biggest wave, and he was washed out of the craft. In the next trough, he swam two strokes to the boat, climbed in, and manned the oars through the rest of the rapid. In a paddle raft on the Cheat in West Virginia, my wife was dumped out of the craft as we careened through the Coliseum at low water levels. We ran the rest of the rapid trying to avoid the raft hitting her while attempting to move close enough to pick her up. "That was fun," she quipped after we had succeeded.

If you decide not to run the rapid, you can choose between lining it or doing a portage. Lining involves letting the craft down the rapid with lines (usually nylon ropes), either with or without someone in the craft. You may unload the gear and carry it around the rapid, or you may leave it in the craft. If a portage becomes necessary, all the gear must be unloaded, and both the gear and the craft must be carried.

Obviously, you do not often portage dories, johnboats, or large rafts because they are too heavy — a fact to consider when you select the craft for the trip and the river for the run. Canoes, kayaks, sportyaks, and small inflatables can be readily portaged. If you anticipate having to portage, you should pack accordingly,

carrying lightweight food and gear in easily-carried containers like Duluth packs, pack baskets, or any of the more modern waterproof river bags equipped with carrying straps, like Ann Dwyer's Dragonfly Design packs.

When lining a craft, you make use of the current to carry the craft through the rapid, controlling its angle and direction with ropes from shore. The two ropes should be secured to the craft so that they will not break free or damage the craft. That may mean rigging a rope cradle using several tie points to distribute the stress. If the lining requires someone aboard the craft to ward off rocks or help the craft through snags or sweepers, every precaution should be taken to safeguard that person. An alternative should be used if there is any real danger. If a lined craft takes on water, it may become too heavy to handle or maneuver through the rapid. It could hang up or break away.

When portaging gear and craft, normally the gear is carried on the first trip to check out the portage route, one pack per person being the average load.

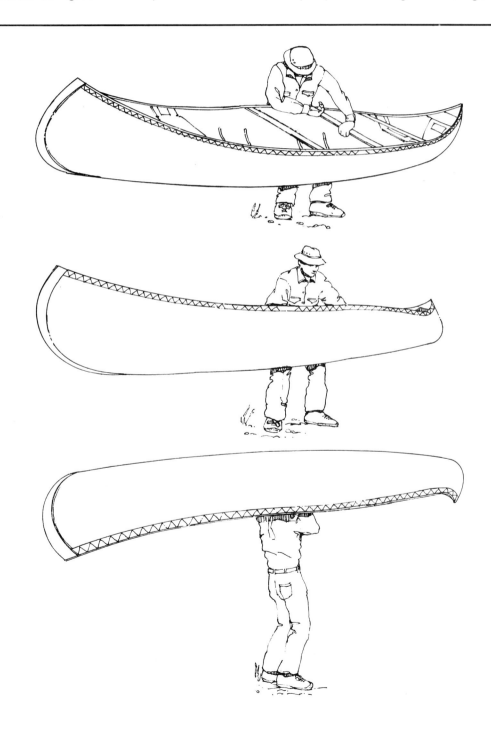

Campsites

The original voyageurs usually carried two 90-pound packs and, on occasion, carried as many as five. If the party has three basic packs, two can be carried (one by each paddler) on the first trip, and the craft and the third pack can be carried on the second trip.

To carry a canoe, use either a one- or two-person technique with the empty craft upside down on the shoulders. One, or two, or three people can invert the craft and help the carrier(s) position the canoe. I like to rest the bow on the ground, twist the canoe upside down into an overhand position from the stern, and walk down the canoe, bouncing its weight on my hands to the midpoint where a padded yoke is fixed. Then I ease the weight of the craft onto my shoulders and walk away with it. To land and right the canoe, I reverse the process.

River campers differ in their opinions of what makes the ideal campsite. Gaylord Staveley, a commercial river outfitter in the Grand Canyon, wrote *Broken Waters Sing* more than a decade ago. A chapter entitled "The Campsite Game" is worth the price of the book. It suggests several elements for the ideal campsite: sound anchorage for the boats; dry, level areas near the water for cooking; screened areas free of pests for sleeping; plenty of wood and water; and fantastic scenery.

The anchorage is important for all kinds of boats, but is more critical for those that must remain in the water overnight. Smaller craft can be hauled up on shore for the night; the larger ones will be tied securely to some tree, rock, stake, or deadman (buried log). For any craft, it is preferable to have deep, quiet water near the campsite for unloading gear. Sloping beaches and grassy banks are ideal. Often there is firewood nearby, especially along the edge of high-water eddies where sandbars develop into low-water beaches.

A dry, level area near the water makes an ideal unloading platform that serves as staging area for the campsite and a place to unload gear in the evening and to pile gear up, ready for reloading in the morning. Kitchen areas are best located near the boats so that the haul from the boats remains short. A breeze will disperse the flies and mosquitoes. When you build the campfire, check the wind direction and anticipate its change after sunset.

Level areas screened by vegetation offer privacy for individuals, couples, and families. Toilet areas are located farthest from the main center of camp. Sleeping areas should be well-drained, grassy or sandy, and open so that you can see the stars and so that no dead tree limbs will fall on you during the night.

Water and wood? These don't have to be available at the campsite since both can be carried to camp in this age of plastics. If the river water is safe for drinking, use it. If it isn't, you can treat it with iodine crystals and vitamin C, carry it into camp from an upstream tributary or other safe water supply, or pack it in. If the camp is devoid of firewood, as many camps on popular rivers are these days, you can collect it during the day and haul it to camp, or you can use camp stoves. The latter are a sound idea as they produce no ashes or charcoal and leave natural wood for native inhabitants.

Some campsites offer special features such as good fishing, abandoned homesteads, waterfalls, grottoes, or trails into the high country. Hot springs make for a special kind of campsite that river parties race toward during the day.

Campsites should be checked carefully for dangers such as black widow spiders, poisonous snakes, bear paths to the water, and moose trails (especially in Alaska and parts of Canada, and especially during rutting season).

AT CAMP

The moon was bright that night, nearly full, lovely on the eddying waters of the Colorado as it slipped past our camp above Clear Creek. I knew the river would be rising due to reservoir release during the night, but had no idea how high a rise to expect. I slept and woke, slept again and awoke to the knowledge that the river was up, but since I could still see the rock that served as my danger mark, I slept again. Suddenly I woke with a start as some metal object clanked against another.

The river was way up, and someone was stirring around the kitchen. Then I heard Rod's cry for help and the announcement that the river was up and about to carry our camp away. I had been sleeping on a sandbar higher than the bar we had used for the kitchen. That bar was awash, and Rod was scrambling around trying to move it all to high ground. Several of us joined him in the ankle-deep water, and in a matter of minutes, had removed everything we could find to a small sandbar six feet above. It had been a close call. All we lost was one of Joy's wet boots, and we found that floating in an eddy later that day. In the Grand Canyon it is hard to know what water releases will be required by Phoenix or Los Angeles.

On the Grand Canyon trip with Rod, I observed his table made from a raft floor with pipe legs screwed into flanges at each corner. Using what I thought was his plan, I went home and rigged my raft floor for our trip down the Salmon a few months later. When I showed up with my table, Rod seemed pleased that I had copied his idea, but he asked about the screws I had used to fasten the flanges on the floor. I thought screws preferable to bolts because they have no nuts capable of damaging the bottom of the craft. I assured him the screws were long enough and well placed—a solid situation.

Two nights later, with the two-burner Coleman stove going full blast under rice and a pot full of curry, someone nudged the table. The loosening screws gave way and the whole meal slid into the sand. Fortunately, no one was burned, and we salvaged the meal, but was I embarrassed! Bolts were the way to go after all. Screws simply would not take the torque.

I ran my first river in 1957, and I have been learning ever since—learning which tent to take along and when to set it up, which woods to use for Dutch oven cooking, what kind of tent pegs to use on sandy beaches, and what rain gear works best. I have found out how to cache food and where to place the campfire, when to pull in for the day if the weather is threatening or the upstream wind is too fierce. I am still learning how to be more comfortable at camp, how to eat better, how to relax easier, and how to have less of an impact on the environment.

EVENING

Landing

Look for a landing that makes unloading quick and easy—deep enough to allow the craft to reach shore and secure enough for safe, convenient unloading. Avoid rocky or brushy spots. Wait until the craft has stopped moving before trying to get out. Don't pull canoes too far up onto the bank or they will tip. Some crafts can be damaged by too much weight in them when unsupported by water. In going from craft to shore, make no sudden moves that might upset the balance of the craft.

The first person ashore holds the craft steady while others disembark. Then, one person still on board begins the untying and unloading. Personal gear used during the day, such as sunglasses, shoes, and shirts, should be removed first. Careful knots make for quick, easy untying. Rafts, johnboats, and dories require group help. If a support craft is involved, everyone helps unload the baggage barge.

It is customary for the whole group to help unload and stack gear before individuals select sleeping sites. A bucket brigade line makes unloading easier. The

kitchen site is selected first, and all the gear, food, and water are located there for the kitchen crew.

Once unloaded, the boats should be washed out and cleaned. Smaller crafts may be pulled out of the water and secured on shore against the possibility of strong wind and high water. Boats left in the water, such as rafts, dories, and johnboats, are normally pulled up on the beach (if there is one) and tied carefully to a tree, rock, stake, or deadman (buried log).

Care should be taken that the crafts and their painters (bow and stern lines) will not be damaged by wave action during the night. If the river fluctuates due to reservoir release or natural ebbs and flow, the length of lines should be carefully watched and the position of boats checked during the night. Boats may have to be re-tied several times.

Some river runners like to sleep on the water in their boats. Small dome tents are ideal for setting up on board rafts with broad surfaces. Smaller crafts can be used on shore as shelter during storms. All equipment and clothing left overnight on the crafts should be secured against sudden winds.

If boats need to be moved during the night, be careful not to lose any gear. If you are in an area where animals might be a problem, secure food away from the crafts to avoid damage from teeth and claws. Porcupines will eat salty rope or paddle handles soaked with the sweat of human hands.

The kitchen should be located near the boats. Appropriate places for garbage, the fire pan or pit, and the cooking, serving, and eating areas should all be part of the kitchen. The kitchen should be set up as soon as the party arrives, even though cooking chores may not begin for hours, in order that supplies are ready and available — a guard against dehydration, hunger, and hypothermia.

The toilet area(s) should be established early to keep anyone from camping too close to this necessary sanitary facility. An area for river games can be cleared near the kitchen for entertainment while dinner is being prepared.

Keep group facilities away from individual sleeping areas. Some people may stay up late singing and telling stories while others may want to turn in early. With modern tents there is no need to ditch the area or remove natural vegetation. The Stone Age of fire pits in heavily used areas is past, and minimal-impact camping suggests the use of fire pans for all open fires, with only one fire per party.

Fire

Fire is no longer an option on some heavily used rivers because of regulations designed to protect the environment. The use of local wood reduces habitat and/or food for certain species and uses nutrients that otherwise would enrich the soil.

Nevertheless, the evening campfire is so much a part of the river camping scene that I do not anticipate its disappearance in my lifetime. Fires are valuable for warming people, drying gear and clothing, keeping insects away, burning trash, and heating stones for a sauna. All are uses that are impractical for camp stoves, which are most effectively used for cooking and heating dishwater.

One fire per party is a common sense rule. Fires should be kept small, and wood should be burned as completely as possible to reduce charcoal remains. In heavily used or high fire danger areas, all fires should be contained in fire pans, which are metal plates with raised edges that contain the ashes and prevent the spread of fire. Put an inch or so of sand in the bottom of the fire pan to protect it from the fire's heat. Fire pans make it easy to clean up a fire site before leaving. Little evidence remains of the camp if ashes are disposed of properly. In some cases, remains of a fire can be carried out with the garbage.

If you do not use a fire pan, clear an area of combustible materials, dig into the sand or dirt as little as necessary, and when the ashes and charcoal have been disposed of properly, cover the pit and scatter any rocks you may have used around the fire. Following that practice, I have used a single lunch site a whole season with no evidence of having been there, even though I built fires every weekend.

A fire pan raised on pipe legs prevents burning local vegetation and is easier to cook on. If river parties collect firewood along the river during the day, local wood supplies will not be depleted. If fire pans are not used, evidence of the fire pit should be dispersed. Ashes can be buried or dumped into the river and unlit, charred wood scattered along with the rocks blackened by the fire.

Fire for cooking requires several kinds of wood. Dry wood burns fast; hardwood burns hot. For good cooking coals, especially for Dutch ovens, you want mesquite, oak, hickory, ash, yellow birch, or mountain mahogany. Different areas offer different woods. Memories of particular rivers live in the smell of a distinct campfire smoke.

Fire for burning garbage should burn hot and fast. Hackberry is especially good because its gnarled form creates air spaces to assure fast burning. Gar-

bage burns best when it is allowed to dry on the fire first, either on the pile of wood or on the grill used for cooking (after the meal has been prepared). The garbage fire, once it has served its purpose, can be used as an evening campfire.

Trash to be carried out can be greatly reduced in bulk and weight, and tin cans can be cleansed of any odors, by first being burned in the campfire.

Open fires are good for heating dishwater, and making coffee. If you cook on the campfire, you will have black pots. Prepare for this problem by using utensils you expect to blacken and by having storage space for them where they won't blacken everything else. It is wise to use two different sets of pots and pans if you also cook on a camp stove—one set for the open fire and the other for the clean-burning stove. Be sure your companions know the difference. Some people soap pot bottoms so that they can be cleaned more easily, but I don't even try to keep open fire pots free of soot. I have learned to live with it.

Cooking

Cooking chores should be divided and carefully planned so that all courses are ready at appropriate times. I like to serve soup courses first. If an open fire is used, soup and coffee can be made while the fire is burning to coals. Dishwater can be heated when there is space.

The main course needs to be started early for it to be ready when the meal is served, especially if using a Dutch oven. There's no clock on most river trips, but it is pleasant to eat before dark. Cook over hot hardwood coals rather than flames whenever possible, and keep things warm by placing them near the fire.

If your crafts have the carrying capacity, bring along a Dutch oven. I usually carry one of the heavy cast-iron cookers, using it for main meals and desserts on alternate nights. The secret to good Dutch oven meals is using heat on the top for even cooking. The common problem is too much heat on the bottom, which burns the food. The practice I use, learned from Rod Nash, is to dig a hole in the sand big enough for the Dutch oven. Then, I place a trio of stones about three inches in diameter in the bottom of the hole to support the oven. Line the hole with coals, place the Dutch oven into the hole, then cover the top and sides with coals. Removing the lid lengthens cooking time.

During meal preparation, all garbage generated should be collected, then burned, packed for carry-out, or disposed of in garbage cans. Never bury it or throw it in the river. Trash should also be burned, but remember that anything lined with foil will leave unburnable foil sheets.

With modern backpacking stoves available, all cooking can be done with petrochemical fuel, but that does require carrying enough fuel along for the entire trip. Cooking on camp stoves provides even heat and does not blacken pots and pans if the stove is working properly. Coffee can be made and dishwater heated on a single-burner, but if much cooking is to be done, a two- or three-burner stove or a series of small stoves is needed.

A table of some kind makes meal preparation much easier and guards against sand being kicked into the stew. Two large ammunition cans with a driftwood board will do, but careful planning and some ingenuity can produce portable tables for river camping. Some parties even carry folding tables while others use a canoe bottom or inverted sportyak.

Dinner

The evening meal can be the highlight of the day. It doesn't have to be elaborate, but it should be adequate, balanced, and well prepared.

Hot soups are a great way to start dinner, especially on early or late season trips when evenings are cool. Use either a single soup mix for everyone or individual packets so that all may select their own soup. Boil extra water for tea, hot chocolate, or any other hot beverage. Coffee should be made by dumping measured amounts of grounds into cold water, heating it to just below the boiling point, adding a cup of cold water to settle the grounds, and then serving. Some people add crushed eggshells for body, some a pinch of salt. True coffee lovers never let it boil, but many river runners do.

Salads are important on river trips to add roughage to the diet. Cabbage and carrots keep better than lettuce and tomatoes. Carrot salad or cole slaw is excellent if you have dressing along.

Recipes

Crunchy Coffee Cake

⅓ cup shortening
¾ cup brown sugar
1 t. vanilla
1½ cup whole flour
½ cup milk
2 eggs, beaten
2 t. baking powder
1 t. baking soda
½ t. salt
¼ t. allspice
Topping
2 T. butter
1 cup granola
½ cup brown sugar
¼ cup whole flour

Mix shortening, brown sugar, eggs, vanilla, and milk; add dry ingredients (may be pre-mixed before trip). Mix topping separately. Pour half of batter into Dutch oven, cover with half the topping; pour remainder of batter on top and add remaining topping. Cover and bake 20-25 minutes. For variety, add raisins, chopped nuts, cinnamon, or blueberries.

Huevos Rancheros

2 T. shortening (bacon grease)
1 crushed garlic clove
2 large onions, chopped
1 green pepper, chopped
1 or 2 cans green chilies, chopped
2 dozen eggs
2 t. chili powder
1 to 2 t. salt
½ to 1 t. black pepper

Saute garlic, onions, pepper, and chilies in shortening, add beaten eggs with which other ingredients have been combined, stir over moderately high heat until done. Serve with salsa (hot sauce), oregano, or cumin. For variety, add taco mix, red pimento, tomatoes, mushrooms, or cheese. This popular breakfast is too hot for me.

Captain's Curry (from Rod Nash)

10 T. cooking oil
10 t. curry powder
5 onions, chopped
2 cans bamboo shoots
5 cans golden mushroom soup
3 soup cans of water
5 cans canned shrimp
5 cans canned clams
water chestnuts

Saute onions and curry powder in oil, add soup and water, shrimp and clams, bamboo shoots, and water chestnuts. Serve with raisins, peanuts, coconut chutney, or mandarin oranges on rice. (Serves 10-12)

Dutch Oven Beef Stew

3 lbs. cubed beef
½ cup flour
2 onions, chopped
salt and pepper
2 T. parsley flakes
10 carrots
6 potatoes
½ lb. mushrooms
1 cauliflower
2 cans of stewed tomatoes
bay leaves
½ t. thyme
1 cup wine
water
Saute onions, sliced mushrooms, and floured beef cubes in beef fat until brown, add wine and a cup of water with the tomatoes and all of the spices (plus soy sauce, molasses, or Worchestershire sauce). Cook for an hour. Add sliced carrots, cubed potatoes, cauliflower, and any other ingredients you like in your stew, such as okra, green beans, or black-eyed peas. (Serves 10-12)

Fresh Fish (from Jomo)

mayonnaise
lemon juice
salt
pepper
foil
dill
Clean fish, leaving skin on. Set fish on foil, coat fish with butter, mayonnaise, sprinkle with salt and pepper, dill, and lemon juice. Wrap in foil, using a double layer to retain juices, and bake over coals.

Apple Crisp (from Sheila Mills)

3 cups quick oats
2 cups brown sugar
1 cup flour
1 T. baking soda
2 T. salt
6 apples
2 T. cinnamon
2 T. nutmeg
Butter Dutch oven and cover bottom with half of crust mixture. Mix thin sliced apples with cinnamon and nutmeg. Layer apples in oven about 2" thick over bottom crust. Spread other half of crust mixture on top. Bake 40 to 50 minutes with coals on top and bottom. (Serves 8-10)

Fruit Cobbler

Crust:
1 cup of flour
½ cup butter
¼ cup brown sugar
Filling:
1½ cup brown sugar
¼ cup flour
½ teaspoon salt
Mix crust batter, bake for 10-12 minutes in Dutch oven, add filling mix to 2 cups of whatever fruit you use and spread on crust, then bake 30 minutes more. Use twice as many coals on top of Dutch oven as underneath.

Alfalfa and other sprouts are great possibilities and several wild natural foods found along the river may be added to the evening salad: watercress, cattail parts, miners' lettuce, and lambs' quarters. Fruit salads should be considered since some fruits travel well and others are available in cans.

Cakes, pies, and cobblers can be made in the Dutch oven, and even donuts are possible. Sweet breads, such as zucchini, banana, cranberry, pear, and apricot, are probably better prepared at home than on the river trip, but muffins,

biscuits, and cornbread are often baked at the campsite.

Common main courses include steak and baked potatoes, pork chops and corn-on-the-cob, barbecued chicken, ham and pineapple, thick stews, and a wide variety of casserole dishes. For freeze-dried foods, add chunks of cheese or a half-pint of beer or wine to liven up the meal. Many dried soups can go a long way for little weight and add lots of zest to otherwise ordinary meals. So can bell peppers. Seafood or chicken curries made with canned ingredients are popular after the ice is gone. Rice is an ideal base for river meals. It takes up little space and is light to carry but expands, soaks up juices, and takes on exotic flavors.

Fresh vegetables such as zucchini, green beans, and carrots produce very little or no garbage in preparation, unlike corn-on-the-cob. Canoe and kayak parties generally carry less elaborate and lighter food on river trips than do rafters and dory parties unless they have a support raft to carry supplies. When weight is a factor, go for the lighter foods. If you have a large carrying capacity, you can easily eat well.

The idea that everything tastes good on camping trips is so much hogwash. Unless it is well prepared, food can be anything but appetizing. No one likes burned hash, or under-done potatoes, or pink-in-the-middle pork chops or chicken. No one likes sand in the salad or soup. Careful food preparation is important. You don't have to be a master chef to serve good meals.

Clean up

Cleanup after dinner is a necessary chore. Dishes need to be done, the kitchen put in order, and food stored away. The healthy method of doing dishes is to use three containers, at least two of them filled with hot water. One is for a hot soap wash, another for a hot rinse, and the third for a disinfectant rinse. Be sure to rinse soap off the dishes to prevent diarrhea.

Griddles and Dutch ovens can be cleaned when warm by being scraped and then scrubbed with steel wool or sand. They should not be washed with soapy water. Once clean, they should be oiled.

Dishes can be air dried, using the table, or log, or the grill which has been taken off the fire. Leave the kitchen organized for the morning crew.

Food can be stored away in the ice chest on the boat or hung on a line between two trees. Garbage should be burned in a hot fire. Do the same with tin cans to rid them of food smells. Just the suggestion of food may attract unwanted night visitors, including bears, raccoons, skunks, rodents, or insects. A clean camp will discourage munchers and moochers.

Check your campsite carefully to be certain that you are not situated on a bear trail. If you are planning a trip into bear country, check whether bears are fishing at that time of year. Black bears, in all their melanistic color phases, climb trees.

Hoisting your food cache next to the trunk of a tree won't help. Suspend it from a rope, cache frame, or a large limb well away from the trunk. Bear problems can be nasty. They are best avoided.

MORNING

Constitutional

The birds start singing before the pale light of false dawn brightens the east. An early riser is up breaking sticks for the morning fire. The splash of water on the surface of the river wakes others as the riser washes out the coffee pot and collects fresh water from the river to heat for dishwater. He or she is not being thoughtless, it's time to get up. Fishing and watching wildlife are often best during the early hours.

Before long the smell of fresh coffee and frying bacon stirs even the slug-a-beds. The camp slowly comes to life for the hardest work on the river — getting up in the morning. It is good to be on the river before the heat of the day drives you out of camp. The coffee drinkers hover around the fire to get their morning fix, and the kitchen crew starts work.

The dishwater buckets, rinsed out the night before, are ready for morning duty and wood supplies, covered by a tarp, canoe, or the kitchen table, are dry. The camp stove has been refilled in anticipation of morning chores. If the party wants to get an early start downriver,

everyone should break camp before breakfast and have his gear river-ready. Since the upstream wind rises by late morning, you'll want to get on the river as early as possible.

In matters of hygiene, don't bathe, brush teeth, or wash in the river. Rather, get a bucket of water from the river. Then do your washing and rinsing on the bank, far enough from the river to keep washwater from flowing back in. If the water is unsafe to drink, use potable water for brushing teeth. Do not throw rinse water into the river.

The longer the trip, the more important hygiene becomes. On a river trip you're going to get sweaty, wet, and dirty. You want to keep your body clean. Wash your hands after going to the toilet. Failure to follow common health rules can result in severe health problems, such as the dysentery known as scigellosis which broke out in the Grand Canyon in 1972.

Swimming (without soap) is a good way to cleanse the body. Sponge baths are another possibility, taken in the privacy of your tent.

Standard hygienic practices can be followed on the river with a few common sense variations. Use biodegradable soaps (I use Mr. Bronner's Peppermint Soap myself) and keep all soaps out of the river.

Saunas and sweat baths are still another alternative. Followed by a plunge into the river, they can be invigorating, refreshing, and purifying. Saunas can be perfectly safe, but there are dangers in hot rocks, cold river plunges, and the shock of sudden temperature change.

Breakfast

Breakfast on the river is an event. It is colorful, exciting, even inspiring at times. It frequently happens in stages. Someone mixes the Tang, another cuts the melon, a third breaks out the granola. Meanwhile, the coffee is brewing by the fire, and three people are trying to balance the stove so the omelet won't run off the griddle.

This first meal of the day is an important one. A lot of energy will be expanded before lunch. Breakfast should be well balanced and well prepared. Juice and fruit are a good way to start. Granola is quick, nutritious, and provides bulk. Cooked cereals go well on cold days.

Hot drinks are good for cool mornings, but not everyone likes coffee. (I only drink it with hot chocolate as mocha.)

Tea, chocolate, even hot Tang, Wylers, or Jell-O find their way into the morning menus of various river parties. Milk is rarely carried in its natural form, but powdered or condensed milk should be available.

Cleaning up after breakfast is no small chore. Everything has to be cleaned and packed away ready for the next meal, and the campsite left in better shape than you found it. The dishwater and other liquid waste can be strained with a wire screen into a sandy sump hole, and the solid materials burned off the screen. The garbage fire should be tended and replenished with dry wood until everything is burned. The sump hole must be buried.

In overused areas all charcoal, ashes, charred sand, and unburned refuse are dumped into a bucket of water, and the solid material strained for carrying out. The water full of ashes and sand is dumped into the river. Great care should be taken to see that the fire is out and the campfire obliterated. Even then you may want to clean out the fire pit.

All cans should be crushed, a job made easier by cutting out both top and bottom. Glass should be washed to remove odors, then smashed either in a metal ammo box or in heavily-padded bags. When we carry charcoal for Dutch oven cooking, we often use the empty heavy paper bags to pad the broken glass. As food ammo cans are emptied, they can be used for carry-out trash. Much of the material you haul out after your river trip can be recycled.

The extra effort made to keep campsites clean does not take much time if you coordinate the effort. It pays big dividends in better campsites. On many rivers, civilization is near enough for parties to dump trash at designated points where it is picked up periodically by

government personnel. If you haul it in, you can haul it out. The extra weight is not all that great unless you have to portage. Depending upon someone else to clean up after you makes government bigger and reduces your options. It also increases regulations and closes campsites.

Burial of garbage is not the answer. Floods uncover buried riverside dumps, and animals dig up garbage pits. In Hells Canyon last fall, we camped at Robinson's Gulch, a favorite campsite, but we were inundated by skunks due to messy campers before us who had buried fish offal on the beach. On an earlier Hells Canyon trip, on which Oregon's Senator Bob Packwood was a passenger, we nearly damaged our rafts landing at Lookout Creek because of the broken glass and rusty tin cans littering the beach.

Breaking Camp

Human Waste

Camp can be struck early in order to get an early start on the river. However, heavy dew and overnight rain can delay the process while people dry out gear and let the sun do its magic, if there is sun. Sometimes it will be necessary to pack things wet—a good reason to carry along a few plastic garbage bags to keep other things from getting wet too.

Tents are best rolled up dry. They can be wiped off while being rolled to remove moisture and dirt, and rolled tightly to fit where they belong. Beat the pegs together to knock off dirt and sand. Aluminum poles should be kept out of the sand to prevent their binding. It is useful to have a personal day bag of some kind along, perhaps a small ammo box or fanny pack.

When finished with your personal belongings, you can save time by helping with the group work. Regardless of whether the trip is commercial or private, your help will be welcome as long as you know what you are doing. The best way to learn is by doing. There is plenty of work cleaning and packing away the kitchen, dealing with the trash, fire and toilet (if you use one) and the crafts themselves—so lend a hand.

Human waste is a subject too often avoided in serious discussions of camping impact. A major controversy rages over whether human waste should be concentrated (as in outhouses, pit toilets, chemical toilets, and natural decomposers) or dispersed through cat-hole sanitation.

In many heavily used areas, river runners are now carrying out all solid human waste, burning all toilet paper and sanitary devices at the site, and leaving only liquid human waste by disposing of it below high water so smells will not accumulate. Two ammo cans (18¾" by 8⅛" by 14½" rocket boxes) are sufficient for a dozen people for two weeks following the pattern prescribed in the Grand Canyon. One ammo can is lined with two plastic bags and a toilet seat is placed over the open can. Only fecal material is put in the can along with a small amount of formaldehyde to prevent the build up of methane gas. As the party prepares to leave the campsite, the double bag is tied off, pressing out as much air as possible, and the bag is stored for carrying out in the ammo can.

In the other ammo can store the toilet seat, extra plastic bags (two new ones for each camp), toilet paper, the formaldehyde solution, rubber gloves (for handling the chore of servicing the carry-out toilet), hand soap, and a small plastic water bucket for hand washing. After each camp, the new fecal material in its newly tied bags is added to the first ammo can for the carry out, and the second can serves as the toilet at camp and as the carrying case for the toilet on the river.

Whichever system is used, toilet paper should be burned. If buried or left, it will deteriorate slowly, leaving telltale signs of previous parties for months, even years. Perhaps the best bet is to carry a small plastic bag that can be thrown into the campfire at discreet times when the fire is not being used for cooking. If necessary, carry toilet paper out with the rest of the garbage.

Leaving your fecal material in a shallow hole and burning the toilet paper may be preferable. Toilet paper may be the single most objectionable aspect of the human waste problem. It often lasts a lot longer than the fecal material.

Minimal impact camping is a natural outgrowth of the environmental movement of the 1970s. For far too long, we have taken nature for granted, abusing the outdoor environment with our insensitivity. Even the Scouting movement has taught "campcraft" out of keeping with the conservation ethic. While some of the rules that have evolved seem a bit ridiculous, the general principles of minimal impact camping make a lot of sense.

Plan Ahead. Plan your trip to avoid popular areas at popular times. Plan foods that generate little garbage. Plan meals carefully so that there are few leftovers.

Control Your Party. Keep the size down, urge your peers to practice respect for the wild country. Keep the noise down and raise the level of awareness about the area.

Pack It Out. Pack out what you haul in and produce in the way of garbage and waste unless it can be appropriately disposed of along the way. This may include human waste, charcoal, and certain non-burnable materials. Clean up others' trash as well as your own.

Use Camp Stoves. Unless there is plenty of available firewood at the site, use camp stoves so you will not have to destroy local wood supplies.

Human Waste. If latrines or cat-holes are used, bury fecal material no more than eight inches deep. Burn all toilet paper and sanitary devices. If the situation demands it, plan to carry out all solid human waste.

Campfires. Keep campfires small, contained in fire pans whenever possible, and obliterate all signs of your fire when you leave. Bury the ashes or dispose of them in the river.

Digging. Do as little digging as possible, normally only for human waste disposal. Do not trench tents, dig hip holes, or level earth.

Water. Do not pollute water with dishwater, human wash water, or the water from brushing teeth. All should be disposed of on land in a well drained sump designed for that purpose.

Fish Offal. Do not throw fish guts and heads into the river or bury them, as some "minimal impact guides" suggest. Burn them or carry them out in a plastic bag. Buried fish offal leads to skunk and bear problems.

Campsites. Camp in established, cleared areas to avoid clearing more terrain. Avoid bear trails to the river.

Some agencies suggest avoiding loud colors in clothing and gear, but I disagree. While they may "tend to psychologically shrink the wilderness," they are aesthetically pleasing to many.

They will also deter hunting accidents at certain times of the year.

The controversy continues between those who would concentrate impact in order to reduce impact on other areas and those who would disperse it to avoid making sacrifice areas out of the heavily used sites. To me, it depends upon the specific situation at the specific time and may vary from season to season, year to year, and area to area. For example, the lunch stop areas along the Youghiogheny in Pennsylvania concentrate impact in the heavy-use season, but patterns at both ends of the season tend to scatter use. Off-season parties are usually smaller and private. On wilderness rivers of the Northwest Territories, scattering impact is probably more desirable.

If we take the responsibility for our presence in an area, remove with our passing any sign of our presence, and leave the area better than we have found it, we are practicing minimal impact camping. We are using the land with love and respect, and safeguarding its waters as well.

Who needs to be entertained on a river trip? There is the river itself with its rapids, swimming holes, and sunny beaches, its fish to be caught, and sand castles waiting to be built. There is the shoreline to explore for birdlife and tracks in the mud, beaver signs, and salmon carcasses. There are the forests to explore for wildlife, mountains to climb for distant views, and meadows to walk through to find flowers.

There may be side canyon hikes to take, historic sites to visit, abandoned mines to explore (be careful what you get into and take along a reliable light), prehistoric ruins to discover, and sunsets reflected in the flowing water.

With all that, there will inevitably be the desire for some group activities spontaneously devised, like the Olympic Rock Throw or simple rock skipping contests. Someone may bring along a football, soccer ball, a Frisbee, even a volleyball and net, or perhaps horseshoes. Commercial parties are more likely to plan organized games than private groups, but families may have their favorite riverside activities.

Some popular river games include the following:

Olympic Rock Throw. A rock six to eight inches in diameter is selected to be thrown forward from a squat position with the arms behind the legs. Each contestant marks the point at which the rock hits. The winner is the person with the longest throw.

Ammo Can Rope Pull. Two large ammo cans or other similar containers are placed 15 or 20 feet apart. A participant stands on each can, and one end of a long (at least 50 feet) rope is given to each. At a start signal, both contestants begin pulling in rope until they meet resistance — the other person's pull. They then try to pull each other off their respective cans. The winner is the one who stays on the can or who retrieves all the rope.

Hells Canyon Frisbee. A natural outgrowth of two or three people throwing Frisbees around camp, this is a tag game similar to Dodge Ball. Two lines are drawn about 50 or 60 feet apart. All

participants but the person who is IT stand behind one of the two lines throwing Frisbees, (at least two) back and forth trying to hit IT. When IT is hit, the person whose throw made the hit becomes the new IT

Several books have been published in recent years on backpacking games or outdoor activities. For several good suggestions, look at Sources. One of these days I'm going to write a book on river games. Send me your suggestions.

River saunas are a joy. Using oars, paddles, or poles, you make a tipi frame and drape tarps around it. You can dig a pit inside and pack sand on the outside to hold down the tarp. Heat rocks in the fire, avoiding any river rocks that might explode. Place them in a metal bucket, using a shovel or tongs, and put the bucket on the tipi floor. Hot rocks can also be placed on the fire grate in the tipi. By dripping water over the hot rocks, you create steam that soon fills the tipi. Be careful not to burn yourself on the rocks or the bucket, and be sure your path to the water is cleared of obstacles when you head for the river for a cold water plunge.

Photographer's Notes

Photo Credits

The first item to buy for any kind of river trip, even if it's only a couple of hours on a Sunday afternoon, is also the least expensive thing you'll ever buy for your camera. An Army ammo box. It is waterproof, quick to open and close, dustproof, and floats even when full of equipment. If you pad the inside with foam, it is kickproof. I used two small boxes painted bright yellow for easy visibility.

Pentax 35MM MX bodies are light, compact, and dependable. A 24-28MM wide angle lens is good for scenery, a 85-100MM telephoto for people and closeups, and a 200-500MM for wildlife. A small, sturdy tripod is essential for low light situations: foggy river mornings, evening campfires, and the full moon rising over the canyon.

I used either K-64 slide film or Tri-X black and white film developed in D-76 with Chrone additive for fine grain. Yellow, orange, and red filters are good for increasing contrast on black and white film. In addition, I leave a skylight or UV Haze filter on at all times to protect the lens.

My camera repair man tells me that "the only reason to bother picking up a camera that has been dropped in water (salt or fresh) would be to throw it further out." To protect your camera from splashing water, cut plastic bags to fit over the camera straps and pull them down over the camera. Lift to shoot.

Beware of sand. Even with most of my gear in ammo boxes, sand was still getting blown into my cameras. In defense, take along small cans of compressed air and plenty of plastic bags.

All photographs in this book were taken by R. Valentine Atkinson except the following:

page 7	R. Hamilton Smith
page 11	David Sumner
page 17 (left)	Kathleen Farmer
page 21	David Sumner
page 28	John Dragan
page 36 (left)	R. Hamilton Smith
page 36 (right)	Larry Evans
page 38	R. Hamilton Smith
page 41	Bill Belknap
page 42	Larry Dablemont
page 51	Kathleen Farmer
page 54	John Kelly
page 78	Larry Evans
page 80	Jim Rennie
page 83	Al Beletz
page 86	R. Hamilton Smith
page 104	Rob Lesser
page 111	Jim Rennie
page 114	R. Hamilton Smith
page 147	R. Hamilton Smith

Color Section

Raft in green water	David Sumner
Kayak	Rob Lesser
Cooking fish	Bill Belknap
Girl in pool	David Sumner
Raft in rapids	Rob Lesser
Lining canoe	R. Hamilton Smith
Canoe in whitewater	R. Hamilton Smith

SOURCES

Organizations

American Canoe Association, Box 248, Lorton, VA 22079

American Whitewater Affiliation, Box 1483, Hagerstown, MD 21740 (Numerous local affiliates in the United States and Canada)

American Rivers Conservation Council, 323 Pennsylvania Ave. SE, Washington, DC 20003

Boater's Guide to State and Federal Boating Agencies, Boating Industry Association, 401 N. Michigan Ave., Chicago, IL 60611

Canadian Canoe Association, 333 River Road, Ottawa, Ontario K1L 8B9

Canadian Whitewater Affiliation, 436 Sitinson, Burlington, Ontario L7R 2N9

Eastern Professional River Outfitters, Box 69, Ohiopyle, PA 15470

Friends of the River, 401 San Miguel Way, Sacramento, CA 95819 (Newsletter)

National Association of Canoe Liveries and Outfitters, Box 515, Big Rapids, MI 49307

National Organization for River Sports, Box 6847, Colorado Springs, CO 80934 (Publishes **Currents,** a periodic newspaper on river sports)

River Safety Task Force, 230 Penllyn Pike, Penllyn, PA 19422

United States Canoe Association, Inc., 617 South 94th St., Milwaukee, WI 53214

Western River Guides Association, 994 Denver St., Salt Lake City, UT 84111

Maps

Canada Map Office, 615 Booth St., Ottawa, Ontario K1A OE9

Les Jones, Star Route, Box 12, Heber City, UT 84032 (Scroll maps)

Orienteering Services, USA, Silva Company, Box 547, La Porte, IN 46350 (For orienteering and compass information)

United States Geological Survey, Distribution Section, Federal Center, Denver, CO 80225 (Western states)

United States Geological Survey, 1200 South Eads St., Arlington, VA 22202 (Eastern states)

Westwater Books, Box 365, Boulder City, NV 89005 (River maps and books)

Magazines

American Whitewater, Box 1483, Hagerstown, MD 21740 (Journal of the American Whitewater Affiliation, bi-monthly)

The Beaver: Magazine of the North, Hudson Bay Company, Portage and Memorial Blvd., Winnipeg, Manitoba R3C OE7

Canoe Magazine, Box 10748, Des Moines, IA 50349 (The best magazine on canoeing and kayaking. Its annual canoe and kayak buyer's guide is excellent)

Outside, Box 2690, Boulder, CO 80302 (An outdoor adventure magazine which often features river articles)

Che-mun, Box 479, Lakefield, Ontario KOL 2H0(Quarterly international canoeing newsletter compiled by Nick Nickels)

Books/Literature

Adney, Edwin L. and Chapelle, Howard, **The Bark Canoes and Skin Boats of North America** (Washington, DC: Smithsonian Institute, 1964)

Atwood, Manley, **Rushton and His Times in American Canoeing** (Syracuse, NY: Syracuse University Press, 1968)

Baars, D.L. and Molenaar, C.M., **Geology of Canyonlands and Cataract Canyon** (Durango, CO: Four Corners Geological Society, 1971)

Carrey, Johnny and Conley, Cort, **The Middle Fork & The Sheepeater War** (Cambridge, ID: Backeddy Books, 1977)

_____, **River of No Return** (Cambridge, ID: Backeddy Books, 1978)

_____, **Snake River of Hell's Canyon** (Cambridge, ID: Backeddy Books, 1979)

Collins, Robert O. and Nash, Roderick, **The Big Drops** (San Francisco, CA: Sierra Club, 1978)

Coues, Elliott, editor, **New Light on the Early History of Greater Northwest, 1799-1814** (New York: Francis P. Harper, 1897) Classic history.

DeVoto, Bernard, **Across the Wide Missouri** (Boston: Houghton Mifflin, 1947)

_____, editor, **Journals of Lewis and Clark** (Boston: Houghton Mifflin, 1953)

Hall, Leonard, **Stars Upstream** rev. ed. (Columbia, MO: University of Missouri Press, 1969)

Hughes, J. Donald, **In the House of Stone and Light** (Grand Canyon National Park, AZ: Grand Canyon Natural History Association, 1978)

Leopold, Aldo, **A Sand County Almanac** (New York: Oxford University Press, 1949)

Lopez, Barry Holstun, **River Notes: The Dance of the Herons** (Mission, KA: Andrews and McMeel, 1979)

Love, J.D. and Reed, John C., **Creation of the Teton Land-scape** (Washington, DC: U.S. Geological Survey, 1968)

MacKenzie, Alexander, **Voyages From Montreal through the Continent of North America....** (Rutland, VT: C.E. Tuttle, 1971)

McPhee, John, **The Survival of the Bark Canoe** (New York: Farrar, Straus and Giroux, 1975)

Morse, Eric W., **Fur Trade Canoe Routes of Canada** (Toronto: University of Toronto, 1979)

Murie, Olaus J., **Journeys to the Far North** (Palo Alto, CA: American West Publishing, 1973)

Nash, Roderick, **Wilderness and the American Mind** (New Haven, CT: Yale University Press, 1967)

Nute, Grace L., **Voyageur** (St. Paul, MN: Minnesota Historical Society, 1955)

Olson, Sigurd F., **Listening Point** (New York: Alfred A. Knopf, 1958)

_____, **Runes of the North** (New York: Alfred A. Knopf, 1963)

Powell, J.W., **The Exploration of the Colorado River and Its Canyons** (New York: Dover Publications, 1961)

Staveley, Gaylord, **Broken Waters Sing** (Boston: Little, Brown and Co., 1971)

Stegner, Wallace, **Beyond the Hundredth Meridian** (Boston: Houghton Mifflin, 1962)

_____, **The Sound of Mountain Waters** (New York: Doubleday, 1969)

Zwinger, Ann, **Run, River, Run** (New York: Harper and Row, 1975)

Books/Instructional

All Purpose Guide to Paddling (Chicago: Great Lakes Living Press, 1976) Excellent book by experts.

American National Red Cross, **Canoeing** (Garden City: Doubleday & Co., 1977)

Beletz, Al, Syl, and Frank, **Canoe Poling** (St. Louis, MO: Mackenzie Press, 1974)

Dablemont, Larry, **The Authentic American Johnboat** (New York: David McKay, 1975)

Davidson, James W. and Rugge, John, **The Complete Wilderness Paddler** (New York: Alfred A. Knopf, 1976)

Evans, G. Heberton, **Canoe Camping** (New York: A.S. Barnes, 1977)

Evans, J. and Anderson, Robert R., **Kayaking** (Brattleboro, VT: Stephen Greene Press, 1975)

Huser, Verne, **River Running** (Chicago: Henry Regnery, 1975)

Jacobson, Cliff, **Wilderness Canoeing and Camping** (New York: Dutton, 1977)

Kuhne, Cecil, **River Rafting** (Mountain View, CA: Anderson World, 1979)

_____, **Advanced River Rafting** (Mountain View, CA: Anderson World, 1980)

Malo, John W., **Malo's Complete Guide to Canoeing and Canoe-Camping** (New York: Macmillan, 1974)

McGinnis, William, **Whitewater Rafting** (New York: Quadrangle, 1975)

Michaelson, Mike and Ray, Keith, **Canoeing** (Chicago: Henry Regnery, 1975)

Mills, Sheila, **Rocky Mountain Kettle Cuisine** (Pocatello, ID: Gallery Impressions, 1980)

Strung, Norm, Curtis, Sam and Perry, Earl, **Whitewater!** (New York: Macmillan, 1978)

Tejada-Flores, Lito, **Wildwater** (San Francisco: Sierra Club, 1978) One of the best books on kayaking and whitewater boating.

Wallbridge, Charlie, **Boatbuilders Manual** (Penllyn, PA: Wildwater Designs, 1979)

Guides

Appalachian Mountain Club, **Central and Southern New England Canoeing Guide** (Boston, MA: Appalachian Mountain Club, 1971)

_____, **Northeastern New England Canoeing Guide** (Boston, MA: Appalachian Mountain Club, 1976)

Armstead, Lloyd D., **Whitewater Rafting Guide: Rivers & Outfitters in the Eastern United States** (Herndon, VA: Candid Photo Corp., 1979)

Belknap, Bill and Belknap, Buzz, **Canyonlands River Guide** (Boulder City, NV: Westwater Books, 1974)

Belknap, Buzz, **Grand Canyon River Guide** (Boulder City, NV: Westwater Books, 1969)

Burrell, Robert and Davidson, Paul, **Wildwater: West Virginia** (Parsons, WV: McClain Printing Co., 1972)

Dwyer, Ann, **Canoeing Waters of California** (Kentfield, CA: GBH Press, 1973)

Evans, Laura and Belknap, Buzz, **Dinosaur River Guide** (Boulder City, NV: Westwater Books, 1973)

Fischer, Hank, **Floater's Guide to Montana** (Billings, MT: Falcon Press, 1979)

Foshee, John H., **Alabama Canoe Rides and Float Trips** (Huntsville, AL: Strode Publishers, 1976)

Furrer, Werner, **Water Trails of Washington** (Edmonds, WA: Signpost Books, 1979)

Garren, John, **Oregon River Tours** (Beaverton, OR: Touchstone Press, 1979)

_____, **Idaho River Tours** (Beaverton, OR: Touchstone Press, 1980)

Hawksley, Oscar, **Missouri Ozark Waterways** (Jefferson City, MO: Missouri Conservation Commission, 1976)

Hedges, Harold and Hedges, Margaret, **Buffalo River Canoeing Guide** (Hot Springs, AR: Ozark Society, 1973)

_____, **The Might Mulberry: A Canoeing Guide** (Hot Springs, AR: Ozark Society, 1974)

Huser, Verne, **Canyon Country Paddles** (Salt Lake City: Wasatch Publishers, 1978)

_____, and Belknap, Buzz, **Snake River Guide** (Boulder City, NV: Westwater Books, 1972)

Nickels, Nick, **Canoe Canada** (Toronto: Van Nostrand Reinhold Ltd., Canada, 1976)

Nolen, Ben, **Texas Rivers and Rapids** (Pipe Creek, TX: Nolen, 1978)

Nova Scotia Camping Association, **Canoe Routes of Nova Scotia** (Halifax, Nova Scotia: Nova Scotia Camping Association, 1967)

Palzer, Bob, and Palzer, Jody, **Whitewater, Quietwater: A Guide to the Wild Rivers of Wisconsin, Upper Michigan and Northeast Minnesota** (Two Rivers, WI: Evergreen Paddleways, 1977)

Perry, Earl, **Rivers of Colorado** (Lorton, VA: American Canoe Association, 1978)

Pyle, Sara, **Canoeing and Rafting: The Complete Where-to-Go Guide to America's Best Tame and Wild Rivers** (New York: William Morrow & Co., 1979)

Schweiker, Roioli, **Canoe Camping Vermont and New Hampshire Rivers** (Somersworth, NH: New Hampshire Publishing Co., 1977)

Scott, Ian and Kerr, Mavis, **Canoeing in Ontario** (Toronto: Greey de Pencier, 1975)

Thomas, Eben, **Canoeing Maine, No. 1 and No. 2** (Thorndike, ME: Thorndike Press, 1979)

Weber, Sepp, **Wild Rivers of Alaska** (Anchorage: Alaska Northwest Publishing Co., 1976)

Wright, Richard and Wright, Rochelle, **Canoe Routes: British Columbia** (Seattle: The Mountaineers, 1977)

_____, **Canoe Routes: Yukon Territory** (Seattle: The Mountaineers, 1977)

Canoe and Kayak

Aquarian Industries, 301-170 Hargrove, Winnipeg, Manitoba R3C 3H4

Bart Hauthaway, 640 Boston Post Rd., Weston, MA 02193

Blue Hole Canoe Campany, Sunbright, TN 37872

Chestnut Canoe Co., Ltd., Box 185, Oromooto, New Brunswick, E2V 2G5

Coldwater Canoe Co., Box 324, Coldwater, Ontario, L0K 1E0

Coleman Marine Company, 250 N. St. Francis, Wichita, KS 67201

Easy Rider Canoe and Kayak Co., Box 88108, Tukwila Br., Seattle, WA 98188

Granta Boats Ltd., West Royalty Industrial Park, Charlottetown, Prince Edward Island, C1E 1B0

Grumman Boats, 7 South St., Marathon, NY 13803

Mad River Canoe, Inc., Box 610, Waitsfield, VT 05673

Mid-Canada Fiberglass, Box 1599, New Liskeard, Ontario P0J 1P0

Norcal Fabricators, Box 250, Callander, Ontario, P0H 1H0

Old Town Canoe Co., 58 Middle St., Old Town, ME 04468

Perception, Inc., Box 686, Liberty, SC 29657

Phoenix Products, Inc., U.S. Rte. 421, Tyner, KY 40486

Sawyer Canoe Co., 234 South State St., Oscoda, MI 48750

Seda Products, 1085 Bay Blvd., Chula Vista, CA 92011

Smoker-Craft, Box 65, New Paris, IN 46553

Tremblay Canoe Ltd., Box 97, Station D, Toronto, Ontario M6P 3J5

Voyageur Canoe Co., 3 King St., Dept.102, Millbrook, Ontario L0A 1G0

We-no-nah Canoes, Box 247, Winona, MN 55987

Western Canoeing Inc., Box 115, Abbotsford, British Columbia V2S 4N8

Whitewater Boats, Box 483, Cedar City, UT 84720

Dories

Alumaweld, 2000 Rogue River Hwy., Eagle Point, OR 97524

Don Hill, 1075 Clearwater Ln., Springfield, OR 97477

Labro, 16311 177th Ave. SE, Monroe, WA 97524

Folding Boats

Folbot Corporation, Stark Industrial Park, Box 7097, Charleston, SC 29405

Hans Klepper Corporation, 35 Union Square West, New York, NY 10003

Klepper Canada (Ecomarine Systems Inc.), 1666 Duranleau St., Granville Island, Vancouver, B.C. V6H 3S4

Inflatables

Achilles Inflatable Craft, 25 Branca Road, East Rutherford, NJ 07073

Avon Inflatables Ltd., Seagull Marine, 1851 McCaw Ave., Irvine, CA 92714

_____, Avon Inflatables of Canada, Ltd., 1410 Speers Rd., Oakville, Ontario L6L 5M1

Camp-Ways Inc., 12915 South Spring St., Los Angeles, CA 92646

Leisure Imports, 104 Arlington Ave., St. James, NY 11780

Maravia Corporation, Box 395, San Leandro, CA 94577

Metzler, Box 15536, Pittsburgh, PA 15244

_____, 29 Advance Rd., Toronto, Ontario M8Z 2S6

Northwest River Supply, Box 9186, Moscow, ID 83843

Rogue Inflatables, 8500 Galice Rd., Merlin, OR 97532

Rubber Crafters, Box 207, Grantsville, WV 26147

Sevylor USA, Inc., 6802 Watcher St., City of Commerce, CA 90040

Wilderness Equipment, 249 Dela Vina, Monterey, CA 93940

Johnboats

Lowe-Line Boats, Lebanon, MO 65536
Shawnee Boat Manufacturing, Flippin, AR 72634

Sportyaks

Dayton Marine Products, 7565 E. McNichols Rd., Detroit, MI 48234

Equipment

B & A Distributing Co., 2310 NW 24th Ave., Portland, OR 97210 (gear)

Cannon Products, Ltd., Box 835, Faribault, MN 55021 (paddles)

Carlisle Paddles, Inc., Box 488, Grayling, MI 49738 (oars & paddles)

Clement, 1575 Rue de Ramezay, Trois-Rivieres, Quebec, G8Z 2H4 (paddles)

_____, Green Lake West, Rte. 3, Box 422, Markesan, WI 53946

Dragonfly Designs, Box 468, Geyserville, CA 95411 (gear)

Extrasport, 5357 NW 35th Ct., Miami, FL 33142 (PFDs)

Hurka Industries, Inc., One Charles St., Newburyport, MA 01950 (paddles)

Iliad, 199 Weymouth St., Rockford, MA 02370 (paddles)

Imperial Manufacturing, Box 4119, Bremerton, WA 98310 (wet suits)

Mackenzie River Co., Box 9301, Richmond Heights Station, St. Louis, MO 63177 (poling supplies)

Mitchell Paddles, 10 King Hill, Canaan, NH 03741 (gear & paddles)

Mohawk Paddles, Box 668, Longwood, FL 32750

Nantahala Outfitters, Star Rte., Box 68, Bryson City, NC 28713 (gear)

Nimbus Paddles, 2330 Tyner St., Unit 6, Port Coquitlam, British Columbia V3C 2Z1

Nona, 1945 Placentia, Costa Mesa, CA 92627 (gear & boats)

Northwest River Supplies, Box 9186, Moscow, ID 83843 (gear & boats)

Outdoor Adventures, 3109 Fillmore St., San Francisco, CA 94123 (gear)

Phoenix Products, U.S. Rte. 421, Tyner, KY 40486 (gear & boats)

Sawyer Paddles, Box 524, Rogue River, OR 97537

Seda Products, 1085 Bay Blvd., Chula Vista, CA 92010 (gear & boats)

Smoker Oars & Paddles, 614 E. Purl St., Goshen, IN 46526

Sports Equipment, Inc., Box T, Mantua, OH 44255 (paddles & gear)

Stearns, Box 1498, St. Cloud, MN 56301 (PFDs)

Voyageur's Ltd., Box 409, Gardner, KS 66030 (flotation, bags)

Wheels of Industry, 820 N. St., Arcata, CA 95521 (carriers)

Wilderness Equipment, 249 Dela Vina, Monterey, CA 93940 (gear & boats)

Wildwater Design, 230 Penllyn Pike, Penllyn, PA 19422 (Pogies, gear & kits)